Fortran techniques

with special reference to non-numerical applications

A. COLIN DAY

Cambridge University Press

Published by the Syndics of the Cambridge University Press
Bentley House, 200 Euston Road, London NW1 2DB
American Branch: 32 East 57th Street, New York, N.Y.10022

© Cambridge University Press 1972

Library of Congress Catalogue Card Number: 72-78891

ISBNs:
0 521 08549 7   hard covers
0 521 09719 3   paperback

First published 1972
Reprinted 1974

Printed in Great Britain by
Alden & Mowbray Ltd at the Alden Press, Oxford

Contents

Preface   *page* vii

1 **Basic techniques**   1
   Flags and switches, DO-loops, packing numbers, unpacking
   numbers, table translation, buffers, open-coded subroutines,
   characters, linear search, exercises

2 **Numbers and characters**   14
   Character to integer conversion, integer to character
   conversion, character to floating point conversion, exercises

3 **Plotting graphs on the lineprinter**   20
   General considerations, histograms, point plots, line plots,
   density plots, exercises

4 **Searching a table**   35
   Binary search, hashing with linear search, hashing with
   non-linear search, exercises

5 **Characters and words**   43
   Identifying characters, identifying keywords, identifying
   words, exercises

6 **Stacks and queues**   51
   Stacks, recursion, queues, double-ended queues, exercises

7 **List processing**   64
   Chained lists, doubly chained lists, trees, exercises

8 **Sorting**   71
   Exchange sort, ripple sort, tournament sort, monkey-puzzle
   sort, exercises

9 **Symbol-state tables**   83
   Simple syntax checking, action calls, subroutine calls,
   building tables automatically, exercises

   Bibliography   94

   Index   95

Preface

This book is intended to help those people who have learnt to program using the Fortran language, and who want to learn more of the tricks of the trade. A bewildering variety of books confront those who wish to learn the basic features of Fortran. Similarly, those who are using Fortran for mathematical purposes can choose from a number of books on numerical analysis. On the other hand, practical descriptions of commonly used techniques for non-mathematical applications are comparatively rare. Knowledge of such techniques tends to circulate as computer folk-lore in the absence of suitable books. This is the need which the present volume seeks to fill.

The aim of this book is to be practical rather than theoretical, to help the programmer with a problem rather than to codify knowledge. The specialist in computer science will no doubt miss the terminology and symbolism with which he is familiar, and the long bibliography of theoretical works. Such specialists must turn elsewhere for satisfaction, since this work is designed for those to whom mathematical formalisations are an obstacle rather than a help. It is a fact that these techniques are well known to the expert, and that much has been written about them. However, this knowledge is for the most part inaccessible to the non-specialist because of the mathematical notation in which it has been shrouded, and because the orientation of much of what has been written is towards theory rather than practical implementation.

Most of the chapters here require very little knowledge of mathematics. It is my experience that a considerable number of people are learning to program whose problems are not essentially mathematical ones. This does not mean that this book is only of use to non-mathematical programmers; rather, it describes some of the basic techniques which are useful to all programmers irrespective of their subject. It is true that some of the techniques described here are more specialised in their application. In such cases I have given a briefer explanation, and leave the reader to work out the details for himself.

Fortran has been used in this book, not because it is the most elegant computer language, but because it is the most compatible and the most widely used. The version used here is American Standard Fortran, as defined by document X3.9–1966 of the American National Standards

Institute (the language informally known as Fortran IV). The only conscious departure from this standard is that in DATA statements an unsubscripted array name is used to initialise all elements of that array. Following common convention, the reading of cards is performed from unit 5, and writing on the lineprinter is done on unit 6. When a piece of Fortran coding occurs in the text, it is often interspersed with remarks rather than with Fortran comment lines. Many explanatory lines in capital letters, while necessary in an actual program, are less useful in a book than remarks in ordinary type. The term *vector* is used to refer to an array of one dimension. Computer storage units are here described as *cells* rather than *words* to avoid ambiguity.

I am grateful to Cambridge University Press for permitting me to use (on p. 82) an example from my article 'FORTRAN as a language for linguists' published in *The Computer in Literary Research*.

This book grew out of a technical report of the Computer Centre, University College London, entitled *Non-numerical techniques*. It will be readily apparent to those who know the subject that my indebtedness extends to many people. I must acknowledge my personal debt to Mr S. Ramani of Bombay, from whom I learnt my first Fortran techniques, and to three people at University College London, Professor Paul A. Samet, Mr B. C. Brookes and Mr Alan Shaw, whose help, stimulation and encouragement have been invaluable.

A.C.D.

London
September 1971

1 Basic techniques

The techniques described in this chapter are basic in the sense that they are building blocks from which more complex techniques may be constructed. In succeeding chapters these basic techniques will re-appear many times over.

Flags and switches

The need sometimes arises for a flag or switch to record the present state of some part of the computation. This switch may be set on or off, and its value may be tested.

For this purpose a logical variable (say FLG) may be used. At any time the value of this variable is either .TRUE. or .FALSE. The switch may be flipped from one value to the other by the statement:

        FLG = .NOT. FLG

The value may be tested by means of a logical IF statement:

        IF (FLG) GO TO 111

Another alternative is to use an integer variable instead (say IFLG). The values 1 and 2 are used. The switch may be flipped from one of these values to the other by the statement:

        IFLG = 3 - IFLG

The value may be tested, and control routed accordingly, by the computed GO TO statement:

        GO TO (111,222), IFLG

Sometimes the need is for a switch which will assume successive values in rotation. Suppose for instance that a switch is needed which will take the values 1, 2, 3, 4, 5, 1, 2, 3, and so on. In this case the switch can be moved to its next value by the statements:

        IFLG = IFLG + 1
        IF (IFLG .GT. 5) IFLG = 1

It is possible to do this in only one statement:

$$\texttt{IFLG = MOD(IFLG, 5) + 1}$$

MOD is a very useful intrinsic function. The result of MOD(I, J) is the remainder on dividing I by J. In this case, however, it is less efficient to use the MOD function, as although the Fortran coding is shorter, the machine will in most cases perform more work than with the two statements shown above. Here again the value of the switch can be tested by a computed GO TO:

$$\texttt{GO TO (111, 222, 333, 14, 37), IFLG}$$

If the switch is to take values rotating in the other direction, e.g. 5, 4, 3, 2, 1, 5, 4, 3, and so on, then the switch can be moved on to its next value by the statements:

```
IFLG = IFLG - 1
IF (IFLG .LE. 0) IFLG = 5
```

DO-loops

The Fortran DO-loop can be implemented very efficiently on a computer, but this efficiency is paid for by the restrictions which are imposed. It is sometimes a disadvantage that the index variable must be an integer, and that the initial value, final value and increment must be positive.

Loops which do not meet the stringent requirements of Fortran may be set up in two ways:

(1) The programmer may write his own statements to initialise, increment and test. The result is a loop which is less efficient in terms of execution time.

(2) A valid DO-loop may be set up, and one or more assignment statements used to establish the value required within the loop. Here the efficiency of the incrementation and test at the end of the loop is preserved.

If a loop is required in which J assumes values from -43 to $+43$, the statements needed are:

```
DO 15 I = 1, 87
J = I - 44
```

If a loop is required in which J takes successive even values from 16 to 2 (i.e. the increment is to be −2), then the statements could be:

```
DO 13 I = 2, 16, 2
J = 18 - I
```

A loop requiring a real index A to take successive values 0.1, 0.2, 0.3, . . ., 1.0 can be produced by the statements:

```
DO 14 I = 1, 10
A = FLOAT(I)/10.0
```

In this case A could be set initially to 0.0, and 0.1 added to it each time round the loop. This would not be so satisfactory, as 0.1 cannot be held exactly as a binary fraction inside a computer, and the resulting error would be increased each time A is incremented.

Sometimes more than one assignment statement may be required. If a loop is needed in which N assumes values 1, 2, 4, 8, 16, 32, 64, 128, 256, 512, i.e. doubling in value each time, then the solution could be:

```
N = 1
DO 33 I = 1, 10
...
33 N = N + N
```

The same result could be attained with only one assignment statement:

```
DO 33 I = 1, 10
N = 2 ** (I-1)
```

However, this would require an exponentiation every time round the loop, whereas the first method only requires an addition. Notice that it is more efficient to add N to itself than to multiply it by 2, as addition is usually performed faster than multiplication.

Packing numbers

In order to save space, several small integer numbers may be packed in one integer variable, provided that none of the numbers are negative. If the integers have values between 0 and n, then the method is to treat them as successive digits to the base $n+1$. This is done by placing the first integer in the variable, multiplying by $n+1$, adding in the next integer, and so on.

For example, if elements 1–5 of the vector IDIG contain the values

6, 8, 0, 3 and 1 respectively, these may be packed into a variable NUM as digits of a decimal number by means of the statements:

```
      NUM = 0
      DO 17 I = 1, 5
   17 NUM = NUM * 10 + IDIG(I)
```

After executing these statements NUM will contain the value 68031. In a similar way binary values (0 or 1) may be packed in an integer variable. In this case the variable is multiplied by 2 before the new value is added in.

It is important to beware of the maximum size of number which may result from the packing process. The maximum value must not exceed the largest positive integer which can be held in the computer being used.

Unpacking numbers

If several small integers have been packed in one variable as described above, they may be unpacked by means of the MOD function. The last integer packed into the variable is the remainder when the variable is divided by $n+1$. When this value has been retrieved, it can be removed from the variable by division by $n+1$, leaving the next last integer ready to be retrieved, and so on.

Using the example given in the last section, if NUM contains 68031, the successive decimal digits may be placed in the vector IDIG by the statements:

```
      DO 19 I = 1, 5
      J = 6 - I
      IDIG(J) = MOD(NUM, 10)
   19 NUM = NUM/10
```

Note that we have here in effect a DO-loop with an increment of −1. This is necessary because the first digit to be retrieved from NUM must go in the fifth element of IDIG.

In a similar way binary values can be retrieved from an integer variable in which they are packed. The only change needed for this in the program above is to replace 10 by 2. As a corollary, it should be noted that MOD(NUM,2) may be used to test whether NUM is odd or even, as the result is 0 if NUM is even, and 1 if NUM is odd. A related fact is that the $(m+1)$th bit of NUM is retrieved by the expression

MOD(NUM/(2**M), 2)

This means, for instance, that the sixth bit of NUM may be set to 1 (whatever its previous value may have been) by the statement:

```
      IF (MOD(NUM/64, 2) .NE.0) NUM
    C             = NUM + 64
```

A similar statement may be used to set a certain bit to zero (whatever its previous value). A certain amount of bit manipulation can thus be performed in Fortran, although very inefficiently. It is vital in all such bit manipulation that the integer variable should not be permitted to become negative.

Table translation

The situation sometimes arises in which one set of numbers needs to be mapped into another set of numbers in an irregular way which cannot be computed. If the first set of numbers are integers, this may be performed by taking them as indices (subscripts) to a vector in which the corresponding second set of numbers is stored.

Suppose that MONTH contains an integer between 1 and 12 representing a particular month of the year. NDAYS needs to be set to the number of days in that month (ignoring leap years). If a vector LMONTH of length 12 is used, initialised by the statement:

```
      DATA LMONTH /31,28,31,30,31,30,31,
    C              31,30,31,30,31/
```

then the appropriate number of days can be placed in NDAYS by the statement:

```
      NDAYS = LMONTH (MONTH)
```

This is very much more efficient than a series of twelve logical IF statements, or a computed GO TO with twelve branches.

Let us suppose that a loop is needed in which the index takes successive values 1.5, 2.0, 2.5, . . ., up to 4.0, then 5.25, 6.5, 7.75, . . ., up to 11.5, then 13.0, 14.5, 16.0 and finally 20.0. This will require five increments of 0.5, six increments of 1.25, three increments of 1.5, and one increment of 4.0. This problem can be coded compactly and elegantly if the increments are stored in one vector, and the number of times each increment is to be used is stored in another. Each time a new increment is needed, both it and its count are selected from the appropriate place in the tables and used. The number of successive values which the index assumes is one more than the number of increments required. This means that if the index is incremented at the end of the loop, it must be incremented once too many times in order that the loop will perform correctly. The result will be:

```
      DIMENSION AINC(4), NINC(4)
      DATA AINC /0.5,1.25,1.5,4.0/, NINC
   C             /5, 6, 3, 2/
      A = 1.5
      DO 1 I = 1, 4
      J = NINC(I)
      ZINC = AINC(I)
      DO 2 K = 1, J
      ...
    2 A = A + ZINC
    1 CONTINUE
```

Buffers

Programs often produce results one at a time, with computation interspersed. If these results are printed out as they are produced, only one number will be printed per line, as each Fortran WRITE statement starts a new record. A better method is to save the results in a vector, to be printed when it is full. Such a vector is known as a *buffer*.

In the following example, a vector called BUFF is ten elements long. NBUFF is the number of results currently stored in the vector, and is initially zero. A new result is in VALUE. The following statements place the result in the buffer, and if the latter is full, print it out:

```
      NBUFF = NBUFF + 1
      BUFF(NBUFF) = VALUE
      IF (NBUFF .LT. 10) GO TO 53
      WRITE (6,23) BUFF
   23 FORMAT (1X, 10F12.4)
      NBUFF = 0
   53 CONTINUE
```

If the program does not produce an exact multiple of ten results, then before the program stops care must be taken to print any partially filled buffer. This can be done by the statement:

```
      IF (NBUFF .GT. 0) WRITE (6,23)
   C             (BUFF(I), I = 1, NBUFF)
```

The buffer must, of course, be of the same type as the results.

Open-coded subroutines

When a program needs a certain process to be performed at several different places, the most common solution is to make the statements to perform this process into a subroutine called from different points in the program. Subroutines do, however, bring with them considerable overheads in both space and execution time. An alternative is to write the statements as an open-coded subroutine. This means that control is passed to that section of the current subprogram at which the set of statements is to be found. When control is returned from the open-coded subroutine, it is by means of a computed GO TO. A diagrammatic comparison between closed (i.e. normal) and open-coded subroutines is given in fig. 1. The variable IRET is used there to indicate the place to which control must be returned. The value in IRET may be called the *return address*.

As an example, let us consider a program which needs to print a page heading with the page number at the top of every page. The page number NPG will initially be set to 1. The number of lines printed on the current page will be kept in NLINES. Each time lines are printed, NLINES must be incremented, a test must be made to see whether NLINES exceeds the limit for one page, and if it does the page heading must be printed, the page number incremented, and NLINES reset.

The number of instructions required for these purposes are too few to warrant a subroutine for themselves, and yet on the other hand there are too many to consider writing them all out after every WRITE statement. This is an ideal situation for an open-coded subroutine. We will suppose that before the open-coded subroutine is called, the

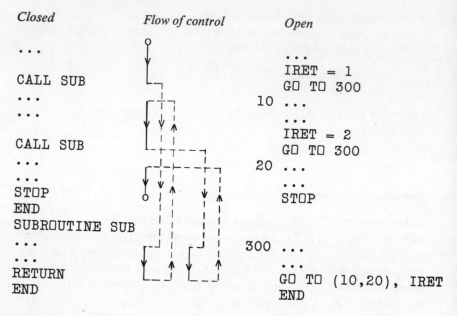

Figure 1

number of lines which have just been written on the page is left in N. Then the subroutine itself will be coded as:

```
500 NLINES = NLINES + N
    IF (NLINES .LT. 60) GO TO 502
501 WRITE (6,63) NPG
 63 FORMAT (5H1PAGE, I5/)
    NLINES = 2
    NPG = NPG + 1
502 GO TO (10, 20, 30), IRET
```

A typical call to the subroutine will be as follows:

```
    WRITE (6,13) A, B, C
 13 FORMAT (1H0, 3F14.2)
    N = 2
    IRET = 3
    GO TO 500
 30 ...
```

Here N is set to 2 because the carriage control character will produce double spacing, which uses up two lines on the page. So far in this example no mention has been made of the initialisation of NLINES, and the printing of the first page heading. The normal use of the subroutine above is after writing out normal lines, but initially the heading for page 1 must be printed before any data values. This can be done by means of an initial call which jumps into the middle of the open coded subroutine – a thing which is impossible with a closed subroutine:

```
      IRET = 1
      GO TO 501
10 ...
```

This will cause the first page heading to be printed and will also initialise NLINES to 2. A branch to 501 will also terminate the current page at any time, and start a new page.

Open-coded subroutines have certain disadvantages which must be weighed before using them:

(1) Care must be taken that the subroutine does not alter the values of variables needed by the calling part of the program.

(2) Parameters for such a subroutine must be left in specific variables before the call (as in the case of N in the example above).

(3) Although it is perfectly valid to call a closed subroutine from a DO-loop, calling an open-coded subroutine from within a DO-loop will involve a jump out of the loop and a jump back in (unless of course the open-coded subroutine is within the loop, which will make it inaccessible except within that loop). Although extended ranges of DO-loops are permitted by the standard, they are in my opinion best avoided because of the restrictions and pitfalls involved.

Several open-coded subroutines may occur in one subprogram unit. If one of these open-coded subroutines calls another, it is important to use different variables for storing the return addresses.

Characters

In Fortran, characters may be placed in variables of any type. (At least, this is what the Fortran standard says. Certain compilers may not allow this.) The number of characters which are contained in one cell, and the number of bits used to store each character, vary from machine to machine. The number of bits per character is most commonly 6 or 8.

The number of characters per cell varies from 2 to 10. When characters are placed in a cell in Fortran they are inserted at the leftmost (i.e. most significant) part of the cell, and any space not accounted for is padded with blank characters. (Blank characters may not necessarily have all bits set to zero.) If a cell can hold four characters, and the character '*A*' has been placed in it, then the cell contents are:

A	*bl*	*bl*	*bl*

where *bl* represents the blank character.

In Fortran it is possible to place characters in variables by three different means:

(1) The characters may be read by format code A*n*, where *n* is any number from 1 up to the number of characters per cell on that machine.

(2) The compiler can be caused to leave characters in variables by writing a DATA statement with a Hollerith constant, e.g.

    DATA I /2HAB/

(3) Characters placed in a variable by methods (1) or (2) may be copied into another variable by means of an assignment statement.

The most common error is to place characters in a variable of one type, and assign them to a variable of a different type, e.g.

    DATA DOT /1H./
    LK = DOT

As the compiler has no way of telling whether the variable will contain characters rather than numbers at execution time, type conversion will be performed. The bit pattern which represents the characters will not be transferred to the cell to which the value is assigned. The convention which will be followed throughout the remainder of this book will be to use only integer variables for storing characters.

Variables containing characters may be compared by means of an IF statement. If the variables are integers, their values will be very large numbers (positive or negative).

If one such value is subtracted from another, integer overflow can easily result. For this reason a simple arithmetic IF should not be used to compare them. On the other hand, some machines perform the logical IF by means of subtraction, and on these machines overflow will still be the result. If the variables contain at least one blank character in the least significant part of the cell, then they may be compared if both are divided by 2. This means that part of the blank character is lost from the bottom end of each cell, but as this happens to both variables, it does not affect the final result. After division, subtraction can no longer produce integer overflow.

The situation is further complicated by the fact that some machines cannot divide integers as large as those resulting from character values. Some of the compilers for these machines will perform division by 2 by means of a shift instruction, which will allow comparison to work successfully. Both division and overflow may be avoided by using a triple test which only subtracts the two values if they are of the same sign. If the variables are I and J, then the test may be written as:

```
    IF (I) 1, 2, 2
  1 IF (J) 3, 10, 10
  2 IF (J) 10, 3, 3
  3 IF (I - J) 10, 20, 10
```

Although there are four IF statements here, any comparison will not cause more than three of them to be executed. Control will pass to statement 10 if the variables are not equal, and to statement 20 if they are. As this kind of test is clumsy to write and is inefficient, a simple logical IF will be used in this book for the comparison of character values.

It should be noted that the result of comparing two variables containing characters will not give the alphabetical order of the characters, but simply the result of comparing the numerical values. Tests for equality or inequality are the only ones which usually make sense in a program designed to run on more than one machine.

Character values may be printed out using the format code An. The leftmost n characters of the variable will be transmitted.

Linear search

It is sometimes necessary to identify a value as one of a list of possible values. The simplest way to do this is by a linear search. The possible values are stored in a vector, and the value to be identified is compared with each one in turn until a match is found.

Suppose that a vector NUM of length 10 has been initialised to contain the decimal digits in character form. This can be done by means of the statement:

```
DATA NUM /1H0,1H1,1H2,1H3,1H4,1H5,
C         1H6,1H7,1H8,1H9/
```

Now suppose that a character has been read from a card under format code A1, and placed in a variable KAR. The following statements will discover which numeric digit is in KAR:

```
      DO 15 I = 1, 10
      IF (KAR .EQ. NUM(I)) GO TO 24
   15 CONTINUE
   18 ...
```

If control passes to statement 24, I contains the index of the numeric digit matching that in KAR. If control passes to statement 18, KAR does not contain a numeric digit.

Another example is the storage of a sparse vector. Let us suppose that a program needs a vector VEC which is 1 000 000 cells long for the storage of floating point numbers. Most of the numbers will be 0·0, and no more than 1000 will be non-zero. It will not be possible to reserve a million locations, and even if it were, it would be a waste of space as most of them are zero. A better method is to reserve two vectors of length 1000, one of which can be called VAL, in which the values will be held, and the other IND, for storing the indices. Initially all the elements of IND are zero. If VEC(264785) is to be set to 3·2, a linear search is carried out through IND for a value 264785. If it is found, then the corresponding element of VAL is set to 3·2. If it is not found, then the first zero value in IND is changed to 264785, and the corresponding element of VAL is set to 3·2. If a value is to be retrieved from an element of the fictitious array VEC, then a linear search is performed through IND for the subscript. If it is found, the value is read out from the corresponding element of VAL. If it is not found, the value is zero.

Exercises

(1) In British currency one new penny (1p) is worth 2.4 old pence (2.4d). Write a program to print out the equivalents of old pence and new pence from 0p to 20p in steps of 0.5p.

(2) Repeat (1), this time printing corresponding values in new pence and old pence from 1p to 100p in five columns across the page, with headings, i.e.

N.P.	O.P.	N.P.	O.P.	N.P.	O.P.	...
1	2.4	21	50.4	41	98.4	...
2	4.8	22	...			
...						
20	48.0	40	...			

(3) Write an open-coded subroutine for adding a datum to a line buffer, printing it out when it is full, which calls another open-coded sub-routine to print a title at the top of every page.

(4) Write a program which reads cards and writes them out until it en-counters a card with asterisks in the first four columns.

(5) Write a program to read and interpret cards containing a three-letter code (in the first three columns) and two integer numbers. The code indicates what is to be done with the two numbers before the result is printed out. ADD means add them together, SUB means subtract, DIV means divide, MPY means multiply, MAX means select the largest, MIN means select the smallest, and END means do not read any more cards.

(6) A friend sends you coded messages punched on cards in the following format. The first card contains a number (in the range 1 to 26) in I2 format. The remaining cards contain words whose letters have been shifted circularly through the alphabet by the amount indicated on the first card. Non-alphabetic characters are not shifted. The final card contains asterisks in the first four columns. Write a program to decode the messages.

2 Numbers and characters

This chapter is concerned with the problems of converting a string of characters into a number, and vice versa. These techniques are needed when reading numbers punched in free format, when manipulating formats during execution of the program, or when numeric data need to be printed in a special form not catered for by the Fortran system of output.

Character to integer conversion

If a character string contains the representation of an integer number, this can be converted into the corresponding numeric form using some of the techniques mentioned in the last chapter. If the number may be signed, a test is first made for the sign character. Each digit is then identified by a linear search through the ten decimal digits, and the result packed in an integer variable.

A free format integer on a card may be read in the following way. Space must be reserved for reading in the characters of the card, and the decimal digits, the two sign characters and blank must be set up. These things can be done by the statements:

```
      DIMENSION NUM(10), KARD(80)
      DATA NUM /1H0,1H1,1H2,1H3,1H4,1H5,1H6,
C             1H7,1H8,1H9/
      DATA IPLUS, MINUS, IBL /1H+, 1H-, 1H /
```

Now the characters are read from the card into KARD:

```
      READ (5,2) KARD
    2 FORMAT (80A1)
```

All blank characters from the beginning of the card are skipped:

```
      DO 10 I = 1, 80
      IF (KARD(I) .NE. IBL) GO TO 20
   10 CONTINUE
```

If control passes from the bottom of this DO-loop, then the whole card
was blank, and appropriate action must be taken. If control passes to
statement 20, then KARD(I) contains the first non-blank character
of the card. A test must first be made for a sign at the beginning of the
number. Record of this is kept in ISGN. If there is a sign, then I must
be incremented by 1 before numeric digits can be identified. (This
assumes that no spaces come between the sign and the number.)

```
20 ISGN = 1
   IF (KARD(I) .EQ. IPLUS) GO TO 30
   IF (KARD(I) .NE. MINUS) GO TO 40
   ISGN = -1
30 I = I + 1
   IF (I .GT. 80) GO TO 999
```

Control will pass to statement 999 if the card contained only a sign in
column 80. Now the numeric value apart from the sign can be built
up in INT:

```
40 INT = 0
   DO 60 J = I, 80
   KAR = KARD(J)
   DO 50 K = 1, 10
   IF (KAR .NE. NUM(K)) GO TO 50
C CHARACTER MATCHES NUMERIC DIGIT
   INT = INT * 10 + K - 1
   GO TO 60
50 CONTINUE
55 GO TO 70
60 CONTINUE
C IF MINUS WAS ENCOUNTERED, CHANGE THE SIGN
70 IF (ISGN .LT. 0) INT = - INT
```

Control will pass to statement 70 if the number on the card runs into
column 80, or (by way of statement 55) if a non-numeric character is
encountered before then.

Integer to character conversion

The techniques of chapter 1 may also be used to transform a number
contained in an integer variable into a string of characters. Decimal
digits are unpacked from the integer, and the appropriate characters
selected by table translation from a vector containing the decimal

digits in character form. The sign is checked separately, and the unpacking performed on the absolute value of the integer (i.e. the value made positive), as it is not easy to unpack digits from a negative number.

When large integer numbers are printed in Fortran they are rather hard to read. We are more accustomed to seeing large numbers broken up by commas which group the digits into sets of three, e.g. 3,145,072,894 rather than 3145072894. The following subroutine will convert an integer number in IDATUM to a character string representation including commas, which is placed in IARRAY, a vector of length N. This character string is to start at position INIT in the vector, and is to be LENGTH characters long.

```
      SUBROUTINE COMMAS (IARRAY, N, INIT,
C                        LENGTH, IDATUM)
      DIMENSION IARRAY(N), NUM(10)
      DATA NUM /1H0,1H1,1H2,1H3,1H4,1H5,1H6,
C               1H7,1H8,1H9/
      DATA MINUS, KOMMA, IBL, IAST /1H-, 1H,,
C                                   1H , 1H*/
```

The position of the end of the character string within the vector is now calculated, and the appropriate section of the vector is set to blanks:

```
      IFIN = INIT + LENGTH - 1
      DO 1 I = INIT, IFIN
    1 IARRAY(I) = IBL
```

Now the absolute value of the datum is placed in KEEP:

```
      KEEP = IABS(IDATUM)
```

A block of three digits is unpacked, and the corresponding decimal characters placed in IARRAY. IFIN is used to keep a record of the next available place in IARRAY, working from right to left. If there are no more digits to be unpacked from IDATUM, control passes to statement 40. However, note that if IDATUM is originally zero, a zero character is placed in IARRAY first, although leading zeros are not otherwise produced. If space in the vector is not enough for the character string, control goes to statement 20.

```
    5 DO 10 I = 1, 3
      J = MOD(KEEP, 10) + 1
```

```
      IARRAY(IFIN) = NUM(J)
      KEEP = KEEP/10
      IF (KEEP .EQ. 0) GO TO 40
      IFIN = IFIN - 1
      IF (IFIN .LT. INIT) GO TO 20
   10 CONTINUE
```

If this DO-loop terminates normally, three digits have been placed in IARRAY, and there are still more to be unpacked. Now a comma must be added (if there is still space), and then control returns to statement 5 to add more digits:

```
      IARRAY(IFIN) = KOMMA
      IFIN = IFIN - 1
      IF (IFIN .GE. INIT) GO TO 5
```

If the comma was placed in the last available position, then control will pass to the next statement, which is statement 20. As an indication of the error (too little space) the section of IARRAY may be filled with asterisks, and control returned:

```
   20 IFIN = INIT + LENGTH - 1
      DO 30 I = INIT, IFIN
   30 IARRAY(I) = IAST
      RETURN
```

Control passes to statement 40 when all the decimal digits have been unpacked. If the datum is positive, control can be returned to the calling program. If it is negative, then a minus sign should be added if there is space:

```
   40 IF (IDATUM .GE. 0) RETURN
      IF (IFIN .LE. INIT) GO TO 20
      IARRAY(IFIN-1) = MINUS
      RETURN
      END
```

Fortran permits a format to be stored as characters in an array. By this means it is possible to change such things as repeat counts at execution time. This is simply done by means of an integer to character conversion. Suppose for example that a floating point number in N is to be printed by format code F10.4, and it is required that the number be indented from the left hand edge of the page by a certain number of positions, this number being held in A. A format can be set up in a vector `IFORM(6)` by the statement:

```
DATA IFORM /1H(, 1H , 1H , 1H1,
C                4HX,F1, 4HO.4) /
```

If this is compiled on a machine which can hold four characters per cell, the 24 characters in `IFORM` will be:

(*bbb*	*bbbb*	*bbbb*	1*bbb*	X,F1	O.4)
1	2	3	4	5	6

where *b* represents the blank character. As in Fortran statements during compilation, blanks are ignored in variable formats. (Hollerith literals may not occur in variable formats.) The characters in the format apart from blanks are:

```
(1X,F10.4)
```

The repeat count before the X may be changed by converting the integer number in N to a character string in `IFORM(2)`, `IFORM(3)` and `IFORM(4)`. Then the statement

```
WRITE (6, IFORM) A
```

will print out A indented by the required amount. Note that for this to work the machine must be able to store at least four characters per cell.

Character to floating point conversion

Characters representing a floating point number are best converted by treating them as two integer numbers separated by a decimal point. If these two integer values are m and n, and if n consists of i characters, then the floating point number is

$$m + n/10^i.$$

The integer numbers may be assembled with no inaccuracies, providing that they do not cause integer overflow. The only source of error is the division by 10^i. The sign should be adjusted if necessary when the absolute value of the number has been built up.

If the floating point number includes an E-type exponent, which may also be signed, then the program becomes very much more complex, mostly because of the error checking which needs to be performed. This problem becomes much simpler when a symbol-state table is used (see chapter 9).

Exercises

(1) Extend the program of exercise (5), chapter 1, to allow the numbers to be either integer or real in form, and to be punched anywhere on the data cards. As before, the three-letter code is to be punched in the first three columns.

(2) Write a program to read numbers punched in the 'commas' format described in this chapter, i.e. with commas separating groups of three digits. Include checks to ascertain that the format of the numbers is correct.

(3) Write a subroutine similar to SUBROUTINE COMMAS given in this chapter which will place an integer number as a character string into a buffer double spaced with blanks, so that for instance the number 67854 becomes 6 7 8 5 4.

(4) Write a subroutine similar to SUBROUTINE COMMAS which will place an integer number in a buffer with asterisks taking the place of leading blanks, i.e. in a form suitable for printing on a cheque.

(5) Print a calendar for the current year, using a page each month. Each page should contain seven columns, one for each day of the week, and should only include days for that month. If the month does not begin on a Sunday, or end on a Saturday, then parts of certain columns will need to be left blank.

3 Plotting graphs on the lineprinter

Although plotters or cathode ray displays may be more suitable devices for producing graphs, the lineprinter can be used successfully when a cruder, less accurate pictorial display is adequate.

The techniques given in this chapter are far from exhaustive, but they are intended to be an introduction to the subject, giving suggestions which can be developed and extended for any particular application.

General considerations

The coarseness of a lineprinter plot may be effectively reduced by increasing its size. It will be necessary for you to know how many print positions are available to you on the printer you will be using, and what their spacings are. Apart from the carriage control character (which is, of course, not printed) lineprinters most commonly print 120 or 132 characters per line, although some print as few as 80 and others as many as 160. Usually there are 10 characters per inch across the page, and 6 lines per inch down the page (often with an option of printing at 8 lines per inch, which can be useful for graph plotting). The number of lines per page can be adjusted to suit the stationery being used. For large size forms it is usually 66 lines. However, the page size is not as relevant as the other information, since a large plot may use several pages, ignoring the page boundaries.

The technique which is central to plotting on the lineprinter is to transform the values (usually floating point) to integers in a range which makes them suitable for use as subscripts for a buffer. This transformation of the values is done in three steps:

(1) Multiply (or divide) the value by an amount necessary to make the spread of values satisfactory.

(2) Add (or subtract) an amount to the result to bring the values into the required range.

(3) Convert the result into an integer.

As an example, let us suppose that the input values range from 5.1 to 10.5, i.e. a spread of 5.4. Integers in the range of 1 to 60 are required. First by step (1) we multiply the input values by 10.0. This causes the range to be from 51.0 to 105.0, i.e. a spread of 54.0. The number 10.0 is used because it is a round number, and this will make it easier to print a scale for the resulting values, as a difference of 0.1 in the input values will make a difference of 1 in the final integers. Now by step (2) we subtract 48.0 from each of the values, shifting their range so that they lie between 3.0 and 57.0. A margin is left at both ends so that inaccuracies will not cause a number to go outside the required range. Finally the values are converted to integers. They should be in the approximate range of 3 to 57, fitting the initial requirements of 1 to 60 quite satisfactorily.

Histograms

Histograms, or bar charts, are the simplest kind of graph for the lineprinter. They may be produced in two ways, with the bars running horizontally or vertically. The horizontal plot is simpler to program, but the length of the longest bar must not exceed the length of the printer line. All that is needed for this method is a suitable character printed using an implied DO-loop which is controlled by the quantity to be represented.

Let us suppose that a vector MARKS(10) contains positive integer quantities to be displayed by means of a histogram. If the quantities do not need scaling because they are already in the required range, then the statements needed are:

```
    DATA IAST /1H*/
    DO 5 I = 1, 10
    N = MARKS(I)
  5 WRITE (6,4) (IAST, J = 1, N)
  4 FORMAT (1X, 50A1)
```

```
***
*****
********
****************
********************
**********************
***********************
****************
**********
******
```

Figure 2
The result printed out for a typical set of values is shown in fig. 2.

Note that this program assumes that every element of MARKS is at least 1, and no more than 50. If some of the values may be zero, then these must be specially tested for, and a WRITE statement with no list used, so that a single blank line is written out. If some of the values are too large to be represented on one line, then this may be allowed for in one of the following ways:

(1) All of the values may be scaled down by an amount depending on the largest.

(2) If the line would otherwise be longer than the printer can accommodate, a line of the maximum length could be printed, the last character being some special one to indicate that the line has overflowed.

(3) A full line of asterisks may be printed, followed by the actual value of the datum, so that the amount by which the datum overflowed can easily be read.

Vertical histograms may be produced by means of a line buffer. The bars may hang down (like stalactites) or rise up (like stalagmites). As the most common form is the latter, a program will be given for producing this. The line buffer is initially set to contain blanks. A loop with a negative increment (see chapter 1) is used to count down through the possible values of the data. Each time round this loop all of the data are tested. If a datum is not less than the index of the loop, the corresponding place in the line buffer is set to an asterisk. After all the data have been tested, the line buffer is printed out.

The coding needed to print a histogram of the contents of the vector MARKS(10) (again assuming that no scaling is necessary) is as follows:

```
DIMENSION MARKS(10), LINE(10)
...
DATA LINE /10*1H /, IAST /1H*/
DO 5 I = 1, 25
J = 26 - I
DO 4 K = 1, 10
IF (MARKS(K) .GE. J) LINE(K) = IAST
4 CONTINUE
5 WRITE (6,8) LINE
8 FORMAT (1X, 10(2X, A1))
```

The line buffer does not need to be set to blanks each time a line is printed, as if a bar requires an asterisk in one line, it will also require an asterisk in the line below. Zero values cause no problem; no bar will appear at that place. Bars which would be taller than the plot appear as bars which extend to the top of the plot.

To produce a histogram with bars hanging down is a very similar process. The line buffer is initially set to contain asterisks (or any other suitable character), a loop with a positive increment is used for the lines, and if a datum is less than the value of the line index, that place in the line buffer is set to blank.

The bars of the histogram may be widened if this is preferred. The last two statements in the coding above can be changed to:

```
5 WRITE (6,8) ((LINE(K), L = 1, 3),
  C              K = 1, 10)
8 FORMAT (1X, 10(2X, 3A1))
```

This will produce bars which are three characters wide.

A histogram is made much more useful by the addition of axes and scales. A *Y*-axis can be added down the left hand side of the page by printing a suitable character (such as 'I') at the beginning of every line. The new format could be:

```
8 FORMAT (4X, 1HI, 10(2X, 3A1))
```

Every fifth line can be printed using a different format, so that the value of the line index is written out. The fifth lines can be identified by testing for MOD(J,5) to be zero. A suitable WRITE and FORMAT for these lines would be:

```
  WRITE (6,9) J, ((LINE(K), L = 1, 3),
  C                K = 1, 10)
9 FORMAT (1X, I2, 2H +, 10(2X, 3A1))
```

Note that a '+' is written out on these fifth lines which is in line with the 'I' in all other lines. The axis and scale at the bottom of the histogram may be written out as follows:

```
   WRITE (6,11) (I, I = 2, 10, 2)
11 FORMAT (4X, 1H+, 10(5H---+-),
           2H--/ 4X, 5I10)
```

These formats are geared to fit bars which are three characters wide. By using the statements given here, the plot will be printed as in fig. 3.

The suggestions made here may easily be developed. Lines and scales may be written on the top and right hand edge of the plot. If the bars are several characters wide, then each character may stand for one unit, and the top line of each bar may indicate the number of units left over, and so on.

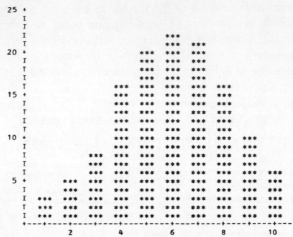

Figure 3

Point plots

Experimental results often consist of pairs of co-ordinates which need to be plotted as points on a graph for visual inspection. Such points can be plotted readily (though roughly) on the lineprinter. The co-ordinates will usually be floating point numbers which must be scaled and fixed as described earlier in this chapter.

Let us suppose that the points to be plotted have Y-values ranging from 5.1 to 10.5, and X-values ranging from -0.5 to $+0.5$. It is intended to plot these values on a page which is 120 characters across and 60 lines deep. As some space must be reserved for axes and scales, the plot itself must be fitted into a smaller space, say 105 characters across the page and 55 lines down it. Let us suppose that the original pair of co-ordinates are in XVAL and YVAL, and must be transformed into IX and IY, such that IX lies between 1 and 105, and IY between 55 and 1. (The larger Y-values must be higher on the page, and therefore printed first. It is convenient to reverse the order of the Y-values when transforming them, thus avoiding the need for a loop with a negative increment when printing the lines.) The transformations may be performed by the statements:

```
IX = XVAL * 100.0 + 52.0
IY = 106.0 - YVAL * 10.0
```

There are two main ways in which the points can be plotted. One is to reserve a page buffer, which in the present example would be an array IPAGE (105, 55). Initially this is set to contain blanks. When a pair of co-ordinates is found (by being read or calculated), these are transformed into indices IX and IY, as above. Although IX and IY should be in the right ranges to act as subscripts for IPAGE, it is safer to test them nevertheless. If both are satisfactory, then IPAGE(IX, IY) is set to contain a special character, such as an asterisk. The statements could be written as:

```
      IF (IX .LE. 0) GO TO 75
      IF (IX .GT. 105) GO TO 75
      IF (IY .LE. 0)  GO TO 75
      IF (IY .GT. 55) GO TO 75
      IPAGE(IX, IY) = IAST
   75 CONTINUE
```

A more economical way of writing this is:

```
      IF (IX .GT. 0 .AND. IX .LE. 105 .AND.
     C    IY .GT. 0 .AND. IY .LE. 55)
     C    IPAGE(IX, IY) = IAST
```

When all the values have been plotted on the page buffer, this is written out, e.g. by the statements:

```
      WRITE (6,39) IPAGE
   39 FORMAT (1X, 105A1)
```

The plot may be surrounded by axes and scales, as for the histogram. It is more difficult in this case to print a scale across the page, as the scale must go from -0.5 to $+0.5$, and therefore it is not possible to produce it by writing out the index of an implied DO-loop. A line buffer must be used, in which the values are built up and then written out. It is also possible to print the points against the backdrop of a grid. This is done by building up the grid in the page buffer before the points are plotted:

```
      DATA IBL, II, IHYPH /1H , 1HI, 1H-/,
     C     IPL /1H+/
C BLANK OUT THE PAGE BUFFER
      DO 1 I = 1, 105
      DO 1 J = 1, 55
    1 IPAGE(I, J) = IBL
```

```
C INSERT HORIZONTAL LINES OF GRID
      DO 2 I = 1, 105
      DO 2 J = 6, 46, 10
    2 IPAGE(I, J) = IHYPH
C INSERT VERTICAL LINES OF GRID
      DO 3 I = 2, 102, 10
      DO 3 J = 1, 55
    3 IPAGE(I, J) = II
C INSERT CROSS-OVER POINTS OF GRID
      DO 4 I = 2, 102, 10
      DO 4 J = 6, 46, 10
    4 IPAGE(I, J) = IPL
```

The grid is placed so that the horizontal and vertical lines correspond to round values on the two axes, and therefore should be placed in line with the scale values. As the data points are added after the grid is set up, certain data points may overwrite points of the grid, but this is no disadvantage.

The main advantage of a page buffer is that the points can be plotted in any order. The major disadvantage is the large amount of space needed.

The second method of producing a point plot is to use a line buffer. In the example above, a vector LINE(105) is needed. As this occupies only 105 locations instead of the 5775 needed for the page buffer IPAGE, there is a considerable saving in space. However, this method brings with it some restrictions. The points belonging to one line must be plotted and printed before those belonging to subsequent lines are dealt with. This means that either the co-ordinates must be encountered (by being read as data or by being calculated) in order by line, or else that all the co-ordinates can be held in storage at the same time. In the latter case, two vectors will be needed, one for the X-values and the other for the Y-values. It will make the program much simpler if the values being stored in these two vectors have already been transformed into integers in the right ranges. There will still be a large overall saving in space compared with the page buffer method. The vectors can be searched for the required Y-values each time a line is to be produced, or (much more efficient) the vectors can be sorted until they are in order by Y-value (see chapter 8), in which case a scan through the vectors will cause the values to be encountered line by line.

A grid can also be produced as a backdrop to the points with a line buffer. In this case the line buffer must be set to contain the appropriate line of the grid each time before any data points are plotted on it.

Line plots

The type of graph needed may be a curve showing the changing value of a certain function. For this, a line buffer is needed. Before a line is built up, the buffer is set to blanks, or a portion of a grid is placed in it. Now the function is calculated for this position, and its value transformed to an index for the line buffer. This point of the buffer is set to a special character, and the line is printed. More than one function can be plotted simultaneously, in which case different characters may be used to distinguish the different plots.

As an example, let us consider a plot of $SIN(X)$, $COS(X)$, $SIN(X)+COS(X)$ and $SIN(X)-COS(X)$. About two large pages of output should be sufficient for the plot, so 120 lines will be written. We will use a line buffer 100 elements in length. The value of $SIN(X)$ or $COS(X)$ will never go outside the range -1.0 to $+1.0$, and therefore $SIN(X)+COS(X)$ or $SIN(X)-COS(X)$ will never go outside the range -2.0 to $+2.0$. (Of course they will never even reach these values, as $SIN(X)$ and $COS(X)$ are out of phase.) Therefore we may scale the values of $SIN(X)$ and $COS(X)$ into the right range by multiplying by 25.0 and adding 50.0. Then the tests for values out of range may safely be omitted. Scaling will also need to be performed down the page. This will give the amount X is to be incremented for each new line printed. In any but the most trivial cases it may be necessary to run the program several times before it is possible to select a value for the increment which gives a plot satisfactory to the eye. The four plots may be produced with the four characters, '1', '2', '3' and '4'. Now we can write the program.

```
      DIMENSION LINE(100), KAR(4), VAL(4)
      DATA IBL/1H /, KAR/1H1,1H2,1H3,1H4/,
     C     LINE/100*1H /
C START AT THE TOP OF A PAGE
      WRITE (6,11)
   11 FORMAT (1H1)
      DO 10 I = 1, 120
      X = FLOAT(I-1) * 0.09
      VAL(1) = SIN(X)
      VAL(2) = COS(X)
      VAL(3) = VAL(1) + VAL(2)
      VAL(4) = VAL(1) - VAL(2)
      DO 5 J = 1, 4
      IND = VAL(J) * 25.0 + 50.0
```

```
  5 LINE(IND) = KAR(J)
    WRITE (6,7) LINE
  7 FORMAT (5X, 100A1)
    DO 10 J = 1, 100
 10 LINE(J) = IBL
C THROW A NEW PAGE AT THE END
    WRITE (6,11)
    STOP
    END
```

Part of the print out from this program is shown in fig. 4. The values are stored in the vector VAL for convenience, so that they may all be scaled within a DO-loop. It is rather inefficient to set all the elements of LINE to blank when only four are non-blank. If we preferred, we could store the successive values of IND in another vector of length 4, and then after the line has been printed, we could restore to blank only the four elements whose indices are stored. If we add to the program above the DIMENSION statement

```
DIMENSION INDX(4)
```

then the relevant part of the program will be changed to:

```
    DO 5 J = 1, 4
    IND = VAL(J) * 25.0 + 50.0
    INDX(J) = IND
  5 LINE(IND) = KAR(J)
    . . .
    DO 10 J = 1, 4
    IND = INDX(J)
 10 LINE(IND) = IBL
```

Line plots can be made more easily identifiable by using, not the same character each time, but successive characters of a caption which identifies the curve. This entails storing the caption character by character in a vector, and each time a character is placed in the line buffer, selecting the next character of the caption to indicate the point of the curve. Scales and a grid may be added to the plot in just the same way as for a point plot. One other modification which is worth mentioning concerns rapidly changing functions. If a function changes only slowly, the characters printed on successive lines will be near together, and visual continuity is preserved. If the function changes very rapidly, the points will be widely separated, and the eye will find it hard to connect them. In that case it is better to insert a string of characters in the line buffer rather than a single character. For a particular line of output, the function should be evaluated for a point midway between this line and the previous line, and for a point midway between this line and the following line. The two values are then scaled and converted to integers, and the portion of the line buffer which lies between the two resulting values is filled with the required character. If either of the two values are out of range, the corresponding extreme value for the buffer should be substituted (either 1 or the length of the buffer). If both of the values are out of range in the same direction, then no characters should be placed in the line buffer.

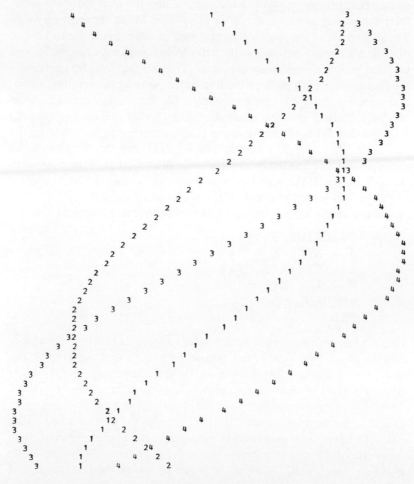

Figure 4

Density plots

A three-dimensional plot may be roughly produced on the lineprinter by using different characters to represent the height of the plot above the page. Characters of varying print density may be used in order to give the right visual impression, or the numeric digits may be used in order to provide some sort of scale.

Scaling for such a plot must be performed in three dimensions: across the page, down the page and above the page. If the quantities to be plotted across and down the page are comparable, then it will usually be desirable that the scaling be proportional, i.e. if there are ten characters per inch across the page and six lines per inch down the page, then the scaling across and down should be in the proportion 10:6. The scaling above the page will be required in order to use the technique of table translation to select a character from a vector. A line buffer will be filled with these selected characters. This will be done by evaluating the function for each place in the line buffer, scaling the resulting value, and selecting the appropriate character. (A page buffer could be used instead if there is sufficient space, but a line buffer will do just as well.) If the scaled value of the function is out of range as an index to the vector of characters, the nearest valid value must be substituted, as every point in the line buffer must contain one or other of the characters from the vector. If the scaled value is too small, it is set to one, and if it is too large, it is set to the length of the vector of characters.

As an example, take a function which is defined in Fortran as follows:

```
FUNCTION F(X)
A = EXP(-X * X)
B = COS(X*3.0/A)
F = A * B * B
RETURN
END
```

This is a function whose graph is similar to a cosine curve, but which is entirely above the X-axis, and whose amplitude and wavelength decrease with distance from the Y-axis. Its maximum value is 1.0 and its minimum 0.0. The problem is to plot the surface of revolution produced when this curve is rotated about the Y-axis. The centre of the curve should be placed approximately in the centre of the plot. If a line buffer of length 120 is to be used, and 60 lines are to be printed per page, then the centre of the plot may be placed at location 60 of the buffer in the 30th line. The initial statements required to set up the line buffer and the vector of characters will be:

```
DIMENSION LINE(120), MARK(6)
DATA MARK /1H , 1H-, 1H+, 1H*, 1HO, 1HX/
```

The characters will be selected from the vector MARK. The six characters chosen are ones which are symmetrical in shape and central on the print line. The full stop is not a good character in this respect, as its centre is too low. An outer DO-loop is required to generate the lines of output, and an inner DO-loop for filling elements of the line buffer:

```
DO 10 I = 1, 60
DO 5 J = 1, 120
```

The centre of the plot will occur when I is 30 and J is 60. In this case the argument handed over to the function F should have the value 0.0. In every other case the argument should be proportional to the distance from the centre point, which must be evaluated by the rule of Pythagoras, remembering that a change of ten positions in J must be equivalent to a change of six in I (the ratio of characters per inch to lines per inch). The distance can therefore be calculated as:

```
  D = SQRT( (FLOAT(I-30)/0.6)**2
C         + FLOAT(J-60)**2)
```

This distance must now be scaled before it is suitable as an argument for F. Dividing by 30.0 gives a satisfactory scaling across and down the page. The result returned by F lies between 0.0 and 1.0. We need a result between 1 and 6, so we must multiply by 5.0, add 1.0, and then fix the result. The required integer value is therefore obtained by the statement:

```
K = 5.0 * F(D/30.0) + 1.0
```

It is possible that rounding errors may cause K to go outside the range 1 to 6, so we must add further statements to check and correct the value if necessary:

```
IF (K .LT. 1) K= 1
IF (K .GT. 6) K = 6
```

Now we can select a character from the vector and place it in the line buffer, so ending the inner DO-loop:

```
5 LINE(J) = MARK(K)
```

As the end to the outer DO-loop we print out the line which has been built up. This may be the end of the program:

```
10 WRITE (6,15) LINE
15 FORMAT (1X, 120A1)
   STOP
   END
```

The printed output resulting from this program is shown in fig. 5.

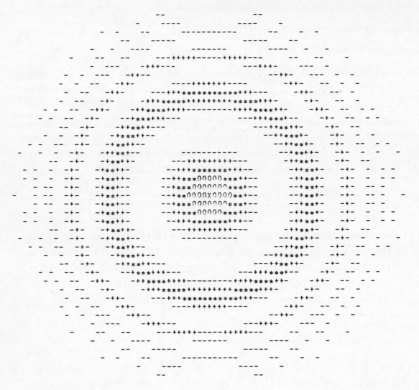

Figure 5

If a large plot is needed which would be wider than the lineprinter page, then this must be produced in several panels which may then be placed together. It may be that a density plot is needed, not of a function but of data points. Unless there is a data value for every point to be plotted (which is not very common), extrapolation must be performed to determine the values for which no data are supplied, but this is outside the scope of this book.

Although the printing may be done in several panels to overcome the graininess of the plot across the page, the most serious drawback to a density plot of the type shown above is the limited number of characters used to represent the height above the page. If the visual impression is not necessary, then all the different characters available on the lineprinter may be used to represent positions in the third dimension. This is hardly a solution, however, as the main reason for producing a plot on the lineprinter is to give a certain visual impression. One soon exhausts the number of symmetrical, central characters which differ from one another in print density. The answer is then to produce composite characters by means of overprinting. By careful selection shades of grey which progress almost to black may be generated. This is done by having several vectors of characters, such as the following:

−	+	*	▯	▯	▯	▯
			/	X	*	X
						*

These may, in fact, be held as successive rows in a two-dimensional array. A line is built up using the first vector, and printed using blank as the carriage control character. The line is built up again with the same values of the function, but this time selecting characters from the second vector. It is then printed using plus as the carriage control character, which causes this line to be printed on top of the last line. The line is filled for a third time using the third vector of characters, and again printed with plus as the carriage control character. Then a new line of values is built up using the first vector, and so on. Obviously the most efficient way of programming this process is to evaluate the scaled integer values for the line only once, and to store them in a vector as long as the line buffer. Then these values can be used three times over to select the appropriate characters. This saves the labour of evaluating the function three times over for each position. A further refinement is to keep a flag recording whether a line to be overprinted does in fact contain any other characters than blank. If it does not, then it does not need to be printed.

Scales and grids may be added to a density plot in much the same way as with point plots or line plots. A grid must be added after the data characters have been built up, however, as otherwise the data will overwrite all of it. If a horizontal line of the grid is required, then obviously no data points need to be evaluated: a horizontal line can simply be written. If the plot is very dense, then vertical lines of the grid may be surrounded by blanks on either side, and horizontal grid lines may be preceded and followed by blank lines, in order to make them stand out.

Exercises

(1) Write a program to read in 100 floating point numbers and plot a histogram of the numbers lying in the ranges 0.0–0.1, 0.1–0.2, . . ., 1.9–2.0.

(2) Produce on the lineprinter a line plot of $SIN(X)$ with the X-axis horizontal. The range of values for X should be from -2π to $+2\pi$. (Hint – use a page buffer.)

(3) Plot on the lineprinter the function

$$\frac{x}{(1+x)^3} \qquad \text{from } x = -3 \text{ to } x = +4.$$

As this function is at times rapidly changing you should add the necessary coding for producing a clear plot everywhere. (Take special care around the point $x = -1$.)

(4) Produce density plots of the functions

```
Z = SIN(X) * SIN(Y)
Z = SIN(X) + SIN(Y)
```

The X- and Y-axes should be across and down the page, and the Z-axis up out of the page.

4 Searching a table

The simplest method of searching a table for a given value, the method of linear search, was described in chapter 1. A linear search through n items will take n comparisons to discover that the item is not present. If the item is present, then on average $n/2$ comparisons will be needed. The value of n is usually large enough to make this a very inefficient method of searching.

In chapter 1 the example was given of storing a large, sparse vector in compressed form by storing the subscripts and values of non-zero elements. Then a search needs to be performed for the subscript required. This illustrates the fact that a search is made more efficient if we use the value being searched for as an address. In this example, if the subscripts could be used to reference the vector in the normal way, access to any element would be rapid because the subscript is being used to indicate the location of the element. A linear search stores items with no regard to their values, and therefore a search must examine every item until a match is found. All the more efficient methods of searching do take into account the value, not to give a unique address, but to give some information concerning where to search further.

Binary search

The binary search technique depends on the table being in order (numerically). An item for which a search is being made is first compared with the item in the middle of the table. If the new item precedes this numerically, then the first half of the table is searched. If the item follows, then the second half of the table is searched. In either case, the new item is compared with the item in the middle of the corresponding half of the table, and so on. At each comparison the area of the search is narrowed down to half the previous area. If the table consists of n items, then the number of comparisons needed will be $\log_2 n$. Some idea of the efficiency of this method over that of linear search will be seen from the following simple example. A linear search through a table containing 1024 items will on average require 512 comparisons if the item is found, whereas a binary search through a table of the same size will only need $\log_2 1024 = 10$ comparisons.

There are two problems to be considered with this method. One is comparatively trivial, and concerns the programming when the length of the table is not a power of two. The other is much more serious. The table cannot easily be amended to accommodate new items. In almost all cases the table must remain fixed through the execution of the program. However, there are many situations where this is no drawback.

We may take as an example the reduction of data to be plotted as a histogram. The boundary points may be at quite irregular intervals, and a search must be performed to classify each value as belonging to a specific interval. The boundary points will not change during execution of the program, so a binary search may be used. The binary search demonstrated here works on a table whose length is one less than a power of two. If there are to be thirty-two intervals, then there will be thirty-one boundary points separating intervals. A DIMENSION statement is needed.

```
DIMENSION THRESH(31)
```

Values must be placed in THRESH which lie at the boundaries dividing pairs of intervals. These values must be in ascending numerical order. The central boundary will be in THRESH(16). The new item will be in VAL. The search is done by the statements:

```
    INDX = 0
    INC = 16
  1 IT = INDX + INC
    IF (VAL .GT. THRESH(IT)) INDX = IT
    INC = INC/2
    IF (INC .GT. 0) GO TO 1
```

INC takes on successive values 16, 8, 4, 2, 1 and 0. If VAL is greater than all the values in THRESH, then INDX will take on successively the values 0, 16, 24, 28, 30 and 31. On the other hand, if VAL is less than THRESH(1), INDX retains the value 0 throughout. The final value in INDX will be between 0 and 31, giving the interval in which VAL lies. Interval 0 includes all values less than or equal to THRESH(1), and interval 31 includes all values greater than THRESH(31).

If the required number of intervals is not a power of two, then the final value should be set impossibly high, so that the search never goes beyond this value. The first value of INC in the program above should then be the largest power of two which does not exceed the length of the table.

If the purpose of the search is not to group values within certain intervals, but to identify items which are exactly equal to values in the table, then an arithmetic IF can be used for the comparison. The coding will now be:

```
      INDX = 0
      INC = 16
    1 IT = INDX + INC
      IF (VAL - THRESH(IT)) 3, 5, 2
    2 INDX = IT
    3 INC = INC/2
      IF (INC .GT. 0) GO TO 1
    4 CONTINUE
```

If control passes to the statement labelled 5, then the item has been found at THRESH(IT). If control passes to statement 4, then the item is not in the table.

Hashing with linear search

The value for which a search is being made may itself be operated on to produce a pseudo-random result which is less than or equal to the size of the search table. This result may then be used as the address of the value within the table. The technique of producing a pseudo-random number from the data value is called *hashing*, and a search table set up by this means is known as a *hash table*. The most common method of hashing is to find the remainder when the value is divided by the length of the table.

As an example, let us take the storage of the sparse vector mentioned in chapter 1. A vector VEC is needed, of length 1 000 000, for the storage of numbers, most of which will be zero. No more than 1000 will be non-zero. We will reserve two vectors of length 1000, one called VAL in which the values will be stored, and the other called IND for storing the indices. In order to find the value held in, say, VEC(264785), we divide the number 264 785 by 1000 and find the remainder. This is 785. The remainder on division by 1000 may in fact be any number between 0 and 999. If we add 1 to the result, the numbers will be in the range 1 to 1000, and so will be suitable as subscripts for VAL and IND. So IND(786) should contain the number 264785. If it does, then the value of VEC(264785) can be read from VAL(786).

The problem which we have so far ignored is that many integer numbers will produce the result 785 as a remainder on division by 1000. So at position 786 in our table we need to store information about VEC(785), VEC(1785), VEC(2785) and so on. Hashing the subscripts of any of these will produce the result 786. This phenomenon is known as that of *collisions*. Two items which hash to the same location in the table are said to *collide*. Most of the complications of hashing techniques arise in methods for handling collisions. One possible way of handling the problem is to perform a linear search from the point to which the item is hashed. For this purpose the table must be regarded as circular, so that collisions near the end of the table will cause a search to continue to the end of the table, and then to resume at the beginning.

The algorithm for hashing with linear search is then:

(1) Hash the item to an initial value within the table.

(2) Does this place in the table contain the required item? If it does, the search ends.

(3) Is this place in the table empty? If so, the item is not stored in the table, and the search ends.

(4) Step on circularly to the next position in the table, and return to (2).

When values are to be inserted in the table, then a search which ends at step (2) must alter the value in the corresponding element of the vector VAL, whereas a search ending at step (3) must also insert the subscript at this point in IND.

Some sort of test must be made to prevent infinite looping when the table becomes full. In this case if a search is made for an item which is not in the table, the search will neither terminate at step (2) (with the item being found) nor at step (3) (when an empty position is encountered). It would be possible to note the initial point of hashing, and when stepping on through the table to test whether this place has been reached for the second time. This does, however, entail a test every time the search steps on. It is much more efficient to stop the loop if the end of the table has been encountered twice in one search. This means performing a test only when the end of the table is reached.

We are now ready to write the statements for the search to find VEC(I), where I lies between 1 and 1000000.

```
      DIMENSION VAL(1000), IND(1000)
      DATA IND /1000 * 0/
      ...
C HASH I TO AN INITIAL VALUE WITHIN THE TABLE
      IHS = MOD(I, 1000) + 1
      MARK = 0
C IS THE ITEM STORED AT THIS PLACE
    1 IF (IND(IHS) .EQ. I) GO TO 10
C IS THIS PLACE EMPTY
      IF (IND(IHS) .EQ. 0) GO TO 20
C STEP ON THROUGH THE TABLE
      IHS = IHS + 1
      IF (IHS .LE. 1000) GO TO 1
      IF (MARK .NE. 0) GO TO 99
      MARK = 1
      IHS = 1
      GO TO 1
```

Control will pass to statement 10 if the item is stored at VAL(IHS), to statement 20 if the item is not in the table but may be stored at VAL(IHS), and to statement 99 if the item is not in the table and the table is full.

A comparison of hashing with other methods of searching is rather difficult. A great deal depends on the randomness of the initial hashing process, and on the density of items in the table. If the table is full, then a linear search needs to be performed through the whole table, and the method is no more efficient than simple linear search. If the initial hashing always produces the same result whatever the item, then again a simple linear search results. On the other hand, if the hashing separates the input items well, and if the table is far from full, then the search will identify most items after only one comparison. It is possible to add items to the table at run time, which is an advantage over binary search.

If character values are being hashed, care must be taken that the length of the hash table is not a power of two. Unless the cells are filled with non-blank characters, the lower end of the cell will be padded with blanks. The remainder on division by a power of two depends only on the low order bits of the cell (and possibly on the sign of the value as a whole), and so different characters at the high order end of the cell will not be taken into account. This could result in every item colliding at the same point in the hash table. (See also chapter 5.)

Values may be deleted from the hash table in the following way. The item to be deleted is replaced by a certain value which may be recognised as a deleted datum. If this special value is encountered during a search, it is counted as a collision, and the search continues. If a search fails, the new value may be inserted in the first deleted location which the search found. Items which have been deleted will therefore continue to use up space in the table, causing some searches to be longer than they otherwise would have been, but this space can be re-used.

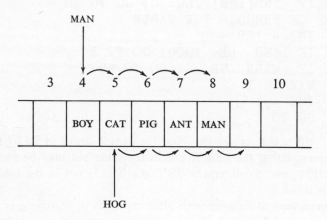

Figure 6

Hashing with non-linear search

One problem with using linear search through a hash table is that clumps tend to develop. The way this happens is shown in fig. 6. Several items have collided on location 4. The arrows above the hash table show the collisions before the last of these items was settled in the table. The arrows below the table show the collisions affecting an item which hashes to location 5. The clump is extended because items hashing to different locations in the same area of the table join the same group of collisions.

Now let us consider the situation in which the search is non-linear. A simple case of this is where the step after the first collision is one place, after the second collision two places, after the third three places, and so on (considering the table to be circular, as before). The items which were in the hash table of fig. 6 have been placed in a hash table with this non-linear search method in fig. 7. It may be seen that an item hashing to location 5 soon leaves the train of collisions formed by items hashing to location 4.

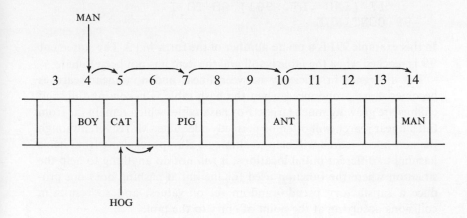

Figure 7

When the search method is non-linear, then extra care must be taken to ensure that every location in the table is visited once and once only in a search starting from any one location. This is not a trivial matter. Solutions have been proposed in Maurer (1968), and in Radke (1970). The method given in Day (1970*a*) requires a hash table whose length is a prime number of the form $4n+3$. An example may be given here of this latter method to correspond with the program for hashing with linear search given in the previous section:

```
      DIMENSION VAL(991), IND(991)
      DATA IND/991*0/
      ...
C HASH I TO AN INITIAL VALUE WITHIN
C        THE TABLE
      IHS = MOD(I, 991) + 1
      INC = - 991
C IS THE ITEM STORED AT THIS PLACE
C        IN THE TABLE
    1 IF (IND(IHS) .EQ. I) GO TO 10
C IS THIS PLACE EMPTY
      IF (IND(IHS) .EQ. 0) GO TO 20
C STEP ON THROUGH THE TABLE
      INC = INC + 2
```

```
      IHS = IHS + IABS(INC)
      IF (IHS .GT. 991) IHS = IHS - 991
      IF (INC .LT. 991) GO TO 1
   99 CONTINUE
```

In this example 991 is a prime number of the form $4n+3$. The statement 99 is reached when the table is full and the item has not been found.

The difference in efficiency between linear and non-linear searches becomes more pronounced when the hash table is becoming full, and clumps are growing much larger. For hash tables which remain far from full a linear search will often be perfectly adequate. Moreover, although the non-linear search will help to eliminate clumps resulting from items hashing to different initial locations, it will not do anything to help the situation where the function used for the initial hashing does not produce a satisfactory pseudo-random set of values, and so results in collisions occurring at the point of entry to the table.

Exercises

(1) Use the binary search technique in writing a program to read in 100 floating point numbers and plot a histogram of the numbers lying between the boundary points 0.0, 0.1, 0.2, 0.5, 1.0, 2.0, 5.0, 10.0, 20.0 and 50.0.

(2) Write and test a set of subroutines to access a sparse two-dimensional array 1000×1000 using hash table techniques. (The two subscripts may be packed in one integer cell.)

(3) Write a program to read in a Fortran program and print out a message whenever a label is found which has been used before on another statement. (When you read a new card, test first for a comment, then for a continuation line. If the card is neither of these, look for a label. Remember to clear your store of labels whenever you find an END line. The END statement may not be continued.)

5 Characters and words

This chapter deals with the special problems of identifying characters and strings of characters in an efficient way. The term *word* is used here as a convenient way of referring to a string of characters, which may or may not be a linguistic word. The techniques described here are an extension to the table searching techniques of the last chapter, and may also be useful to the programmer whose data consist of strings of items which are not characters.

Identifying characters

In order to identify individual characters in the data, it is necessary to read them by A1 format. The techniques of linear search, binary search or hashing may then be used to identify them. Linear search is the simplest and also the least efficient method, and should be used when the number of possible characters is small, and the search is not being made many times. Binary search requires the characters to be in numerical order in the table. This may be done by setting up the character values by means of Hollerith constants in a DATA statement, and then sorting these into numerical order (see chapter 8). It must not be assumed that the alphabetical characters are in ascending numerical order when they are in alphabetical order: on some machines this is not so, as some of the characters when stored in integer cells will be positive and some negative.

Hashing by division will only work if the machine is capable of dividing integers as large as those resulting from character values. Surprisingly enough, not all machines are capable of this. After this hurdle has been overcome, one must face the problem that MOD(M, N) where M is negative gives different results on different compilers. Some give a positive result (which is more useful), and others a negative one (which agrees with the standard for Fortran). If the result is negative, then N must be added to it to make it positive. Then a search can be made through a hash table. As the number of characters which can be represented in a computer is never very large, the hash table can easily be constructed large enough for collisions to be infrequent, and therefore for the search to be efficient.

It is also possible to hash characters in such a way that collisions cannot occur. Suppose that the variable I contains a character read in by A1 format. Then the assignment statement

$$J = I - (I/257)*257 + 257$$

will (for most machines) place in J a value between 1 and 513 which is unique for that character on that machine (although the same character will, of course, give different results on different machines). This method of hashing will only work on a machine which can multiply and divide character values held in integer cells.

Some readers may wonder why the expression given above will hash characters without collision. This may be proved for characters which result in positive integer values by showing that two values can only be congruent modulo 257 if the bit patterns for the leftmost characters are congruent modulo 257. As machines use at most eight bits to store a character, such characters can only be congruent if they are identical (see Day (1971), pp. 255–6). The proof may then be extended to characters giving negative integers. In this case the two situations of machines which round down and machines which round towards zero on division must be considered.

If a program is being written which will be run on machines which hold characters in six bits, then the hashing function may be changed to

$$J = I - (I/65)*65 + 65$$

which gives results lying between 1 and 129.

The purpose of all methods of identifying characters is to reduce the huge and unwieldy number which is the character to a small positive integer value. This value will usually be the index of the cell in the search table at which the character was found. If another vector of the same length as the search table is used, then by table translation the index can be transformed to another integer which may be more convenient in some way, such as being smaller in magnitude. This is especially important with hashing techniques, when the hash table is larger than the number of characters, and therefore the indices obtained are not contiguous. Another convenience may be that the new integer indicates the desired index of the character in an alphabetical list, i.e. the index of the character in a *collating sequence*. The smaller integers obtained by table translation may be packed several to a cell for more efficient processing, and later unpacked for printing. In order to obtain the character values once more from the small integer values, a vector of characters in collating sequence order is accessed by means of table translation.

Identifying keywords

The term *keyword* is used here to mean character strings which are known at the time the program is written, and which are usually few in number. If the keywords are all the same length, then they may be stored in a two-dimensional array. A word in the data may be identified by performing a linear search through the keywords. If the number of keywords is small, then this is perfectly adequate. If the keyword in the data must always appear in the same columns, then it may be read by A*n* format, where *n* is greater than 1, and compared against copies of the keywords held in the same way in an array. If, however, the keyword may appear in the data in free format, the format code A1 must be used.

As an example, let us suppose that columns 1 to 4 of a data card contain a keyword which may be SORT, TEXT or STOP. Format code A1 will be used here because of its greater generality. The card may be read and the keyword identified by means of the statements:

```
      DIMENSION KARD(80), KEY(4,3)
      DATA KEY /1HS,1HO,1HR,1HT,1HT,1HE,
     C           1HX,1HT,1HS,1HT,1HO,1HP/
      READ (5,13) KARD
   13 FORMAT (80A1)
      DO 17 I = 1, 3
      DO 15 J = 1, 4
      IF (KARD(J) .NE. KEY(J,I)) GO TO 17
   15 CONTINUE
      GO TO 23
   17 CONTINUE
```

If control passes to statement 23, then the keyword has been successfully identified, and I contains 1, 2 or 3 to indicate whether the keyword was SORT, TEXT or STOP. If control passes through statement 17, then the card is wrongly punched, and does not contain any of these three keywords.

If the keywords are not of the same length, they may be stored in a two-dimensional array together with their lengths. This means that the space reserved for every keyword must be the same as that reserved for the longest, and therefore some space will be wasted.

As an example, let us suppose that the data card contains (beginning in column 1) a keyword which may be DO, STOP or END. The lengths of the keywords are stored in the same array as the characters. Before attempting to identify a keyword, its length is taken from the array, and that number of characters compared:

```
      DIMENSION KARD(80), KEY(5,3)
      DATA KEY /2, 1HD, 1HO, 2*0,
     C           4, 1HS, 1HT, 1HO, 1HP,
     C           3, 1HE, 1HN, 1HD, 0/
      READ (5,13) KARD
   13 FORMAT (80A1)
      DO 17 I = 1, 3
      N = KEY(1, I)
      DO 15 J = 1, N
      IF (KARD(J) .NE. KEY(J+1, I)) GO TO 17
   15 CONTINUE
      GO TO 23
   17 CONTINUE
```

The wastage of space in this method may be a considerable disadvantage in certain cases. If, for instance, the keywords being identified are those of Fortran itself, then all keywords must be given the same space as DOUBLEPRECISION, which is the longest. A more economical method of storage is to place the keywords in a vector, preceded by their lengths, and to leapfrog over them until a match is found.

If the keywords are as before, DO, STOP and END, then the corresponding statements are:

```
      DIMENSION KARD(80), KEY(12)
      DATA KEY /2, 1HD, 1HO,
     C           4, 1HS, 1HT, 1HO, 1HP,
     C           3, 1HE, 1HN, 1HD/
      READ (5,13) KARD
   13 FORMAT (80A1)
      INDX = 1
      DO 17 I = 1, 3
C FIND THE LENGTH OF THE NEXT KEYWORD
      N = KEY(INDX)
C MATCH THE CHARACTERS OF THIS KEYWORD
      DO 15 J = 1, N
      IND = INDX + J
```

```
     IF (KARD(J) .NE. KEY(IND)) GO TO 17
  15 CONTINUE
C LEAPFROG TO THE NEXT KEYWORD
  17 INDX = INDX + N + 1
```

Here INDX is the position in KEY at which the length of the current keyword is stored. IND is the position in KEY of the character currently being compared with a character of the card.

When keywords are of different lengths, the situation may arise where one keyword is identical to the first part of another keyword, as, for instance, in Fortran, where END is included in ENDFILE, DO in DOUBLEPRECISION. In such cases it is important to attempt to identify the longer keyword before the shorter, included one, as otherwise the shorter keyword will always be found, and the longer one will never be considered. (This problem is overcome in a different manner in chapter 9.)

Identifying words

The previous section assumed that the strings to be identified were few in number and were known when the program was written. These two conditions are not always fulfilled. An example would be the production of a frequency count of words in a piece of natural language text material. In this kind of situation the use of a two-dimensional array is especially wasteful, as each word must be given the same space as the longest, and the length of the longest will not be known until the count is performed. To be safe, the length must be overestimated. Furthermore, there will be a large number of different words, each of which must have the same space, and the total wastage is therefore very great.

For these reasons it is much better to store the words in a vector preceded by their lengths. A further economy in space is achieved by transforming the characters into small integer numbers and packing these into the cells of the vector. The length of each word will then be not the number of characters in the word, but the number of cells needed to store it. A diagrammatic representation of part of such a vector is shown here:

1	THE	2	MOL	E	3	WOR	KIN	G	2	VER	Y

Note that this is diagrammatic because the characters are not in fact stored, but only packed integers representing the characters. When a word is encountered in the data, the method is as follows. The word is packed into a short work vector, with its length. (The end of the word can presumably be detected by scanning for a blank or a punctuation mark.) Then a linear search is made through the main vector until a word is found which matches both the length and the characters. If no match is found, the new word is transferred from the work vector to the first available locations in the main vector. Either a count is kept of the number of locations in the main vector which have been used, or the cell immediately following the last word stored is set to zero. In the latter case, when the linear search is being made, a length of zero means that all of the words already stored have been considered, and none of them match the new word.

A linear search of this kind through a large number of words is very slow. On the other hand, the words cannot be placed in a hash table very easily because they are of different lengths. We could place them in a hash table if we are prepared to reserve the same space for each of them, but this has been ruled out. However, the advantages of both the speed of a hash table and the economy of storage by using a long vector can be combined if the hash table contains pointers to the vector. This means that at a certain location in the hash table there is stored the index at which the word can be found in the vector. This is shown diagrammatically in fig. 8. When a word is encountered in the data, it is packed into a short work vector as before. Then the word as a whole is hashed to give an initial point in the hash table, from which the search begins. If the cell of the hash table is empty, then the word has not been stored, and it may then be added to the word vector, with a pointer to it from the hash table. If the cell of the hash table is not empty, its contents give an index to the word vector. The new word is matched (in length and characters) with the word in the vector. If a mismatch is found, then a collision has occurred, and the search through the hash table continues.

In most cases some other information about the words must be stored, e.g. the number of times a particular word has occurred. This could be stored in a vector parallel to the hash table, but as the hash table will not be completely filled, nor will the parallel vector, and wastage of space will result. A better solution is to store the information in the long vector. Each word will then be represented by one cell for the length, several cells for the characters, and then a fixed number of cells for the extra information. The starting point of these extra cells can be found from the beginning of the word by using the length.

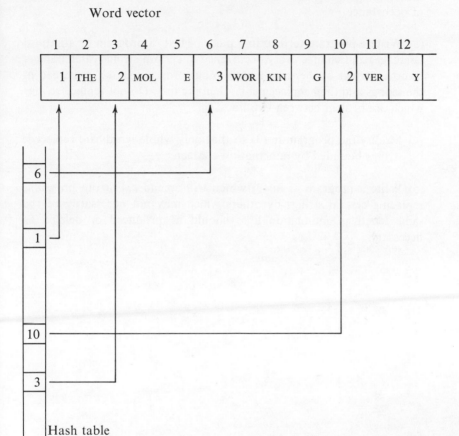

Figure 8

Exercises

(1) Write a program to read in a Fortran program and count the number of times each keyword occurs starting in column 7. Assume that the keywords are punched with no intervening blanks except for the keyword GO TO. Also assume that no variable which is identical with a keyword, or whose beginning is identical with a keyword, will start in column 7.

(2) Write a program to produce a frequency count of words in natural

text. The punctuation marks assumed should be blank, comma and full stop. The output should print the word followed by its frequency of occurrence.

(3) Write a program to read in a piece of text (a program or a natural language) and change every occurrence of certain strings of characters to other strings of the same length. Your program should first read in the strings and their replacements, then the text. Do not replace strings which are broken between two lines.

(4) Modify the program in (3) so that only whole words are replaced, i.e. strings bounded by punctuation characters.

(5) Write a program as in (3) which will amend a Fortran program, replacing certain strings by others which may not necessarily be the same length. Continuation lines should be produced or deleted as necessary.

6 Stacks and queues

The terms *stack* and *queue* refer to ways of keeping data in particular relations to one another. Both can be implemented fairly simply in Fortran by means of a vector. The application of stacks to recursion is such an important topic that a special section has been devoted to this.

Stacks

A stack is a list of items which are held in such a way that the items are retrieved in the reverse order to that in which they were stored. For this reason, a stack is often known as a last-in-first-out list, or a pushdown store. In Fortran a stack can be implemented by means of a vector and a pointer. The vector should, of course, be of the same type as the data items. The pointer is an integer variable which holds the index of the last item placed in the vector. When the stack is empty, the pointer may be set to zero. Items are added to ('pushed down on') the stack by incrementing the pointer and placing the new item at the location within the vector indicated by the pointer. A value is removed ('popped up') from the stack by taking it from the position in the vector indicated by the pointer, and decrementing the pointer. Tests need to be incorporated to ensure that no more values are pushed down on the stack than the vector can accommodate, and on the other hand that no attempts are made to pop values from the stack when it is already empty.

If the vector is set up by the statement

        DIMENSION IVEC(100)

and the pointer is IPT, then the value contained in I may be pushed down on the stack by the statements:

        IPT = IPT + 1
        IF (IPT .LE. 100) GO TO 3
        WRITE (6,55)
     55 FORMAT (27H ***STACK HAS OVERFLOWED***)

```
      STOP
    3 IVEC(IPT) = I
```

The item currently on the 'top' of the stack may be popped and the value placed in I by means of the statements:

```
      IF (IPT .GT. 0) GO TO 5
      WRITE (6,77)
   77 FORMAT (28H ***STACK HAS UNDERFLOWED***)
      STOP
    5 I = IVEC(IPT)
      IPT = IPT - 1
```

The situation sometimes arises where sets of values are to be pushed down on a stack. This can be handled by means of several vectors, all of which are controlled by the same pointer. The vectors may, of course, be of different types, depending on the types of the items in each set of values. If the items are all of the same type, then it is possible to use one vector. For instance, if three integer values make up one set, then the three may be pushed down on the same vector and popped up at the same time. If the sets of items are variable in number, but are all of the same type, they may be pushed down on one vector followed by the count of the number of items in the set, which is also pushed down. The number of items is then popped first when the set is being retrieved.

Recursion

Recursive calls to functions and subroutines (whether directly or indirectly recursive) are forbidden in Fortran. This means that a subprogram may not call itself. Nor may it call another subprogram which then calls the first one. This is sometimes a drawback, as there are some problems which become much simpler when they are phrased in a recursive form. It is, however, possible to code these problems in Fortran in such a way that their recursive nature is preserved, and yet the rules of Fortran are not violated.

First it is necessary to understand why Fortran forbids recursive calls. When a subroutine or function is called, the return address is stored. This is the address within the calling subprogram to which control is to be handed when a RETURN statement is obeyed. The subroutine or function only stores one return address at a time. This makes a recursive call impossible, because a stack of return addresses would be needed to return correctly from such a call. Another problem is that when a lower level subprogram is called, the variables in the calling program should not be changed unless they are parameters or are in common. If the called subprogram calls the calling subprogram, or itself, in a recursive manner, then the previous values of all variables used must be stored on a stack so that they may be restored when the recursive call is ended.

Despite these problems, a recursive procedure may be written in Fortran if it is done as an open-coded subroutine (see chapter 1). A stack is needed for the parameters, the return address, and for any variables whose values must be preserved and restored when the recursive call is over. The latter will be called *local* variables.

The basic features of recursive programming using an open-coded subroutine and a stack may be listed here:

(1) The stack is controlled by one pointer, and has separate vectors for (*a*) each parameter, (*b*) the return address and (*c*) each local variable. The stack is initially empty.

(2) A call to the procedure involves pushing down the parameters, the return address and the local variables on the stack, and branching to the open-coded subroutine.

(3) Inside the open-coded subroutine every reference to a parameter or to a local variable must be a reference to the value on the top of the corresponding vector of the stack.

(4) If the procedure is to take the place of a function, i.e. if it is to return a single value as its result, this value must be left in a certain variable before the return takes place.

(5) Control is returned from the procedure by popping the return address from the top of the stack (which will also pop the parameters and local variables), and branching to the statement corresponding to the return address.

The return address may in fact be an integer flag on which a computed GO TO is based, as it was in the simple open-coded subroutine described in chapter 1.

One of the simplest examples of a recursively defined function is the factorial. If recursive function calls could be made in Fortran, then a program could be written to evaluate factorials in this way. The following statements show how this would be done, but as this would be illegal Fortran, each statement has been made into a comment.

```
C       J = IFACT(7)
        ...
C       FUNCTION IFACT(N)
C       IF (N .GT. 1) GO TO 177
C       IFACT = 1
C       GO TO 199
C 177   IFACT = N * IFACT(N-1)
C 199   RETURN
C       END
```

The illegal function above may be written quite legally as a recursively-called open-coded subroutine. The stack will have vectors NVEC (for values of the parameter N) and IRTVEC (for the return addresses). No local variables are used here. The stack pointer will be the variable IPT. The value of the function will be left in a variable called IFACT. The initial statements to set up the stack will be:

```
DIMENSION NVEC(10), IRTVEC(10)
DATA IPT /0/
```

Corresponding to the statement which calls IFACT with an argument of 7 and places the result in J, we will have statements which push down the parameter and the return address on the stack, branch to the open-coded subroutine, and on return from there place the value which has been calculated into J:

```
      IPT = IPT + 1
      NVEC(IPT) = 7
      IRTVEC(IPT) = 1
      GO TO 155
   10 J = IFACT
```

In the open-coded subroutine the first thing to do is to test whether the parameter is 1. If it is, then IFACT is set to 1, and a branch is made to the return coding. In testing the parameter we must test the item on the top of the stack:

```
155 IF (NVEC(IPT) .GT. 1) GO TO 177
    IFACT = 1
    GO TO 199
```

If the parameter was not 1, a recursive call must be made to the open-coded subroutine. This involves pushing down the new parameter and return address on the stack. The new parameter is the old parameter minus 1. On return from the recursive call, the old parameter (which will once again be on top of the stack) must be multiplied by the result of the function, which is in `IFACT`:

```
177 IPT = IPT + 1
    NVEC(IPT) = NVEC(IPT-1) - 1
    IRTVEC(IPT) = 2
    GO TO 155
 20 IFACT = NVEC(IPT) * IFACT
```

Now the return coding must be inserted. The return address must be taken from the stack, the stack pointer decremented, and return made to the appropriate place:

```
199 IRT = IRTVEC(IPT)
    IPT = IPT - 1
    GO TO (10, 20), IRT
    END
```

For brevity, the test for stack overflow has been omitted. This should be inserted after statement `177`.

A more searching test of a recursive mechanism is provided by Ackerman's function. This function, $A(m, n)$, may be defined in Algol terms as:

> **if** $m=0$ **then** $n+1$
> > **else if** $n=0$ **then** $A\,(m-1, 1)$
> > > **else** $A\,(m-1, A\,(m, n-1))$

(It is hoped that this definition will be self-explanatory even to those who do not know any Algol.) This function will now be written in Fortran using the technique described above. A stack will be needed to store the two parameters and the return address. For this purpose three vectors will be used, called `MVEC`, `NVEC` and `IRTVEC`. It is convenient (though not vital) to use a subroutine for pushing down parameters and return addresses on the stack. The following subroutine will be used:

```
      SUBROUTINE PUSH (M, N, IRET)
      COMMON IPT, MVEC(100), NVEC(100),
   C              IRTVEC(100)
      IPT = IPT + 1
      IF (IPT .LE. 100) GO TO 1
```

```
      WRITE (6,2)
    2 FORMAT (20H ***STACK IS FULL***)
      STOP
    1 MVEC(IPT) = M
      NVEC(IPT) = N
      IRTVEC(IPT) = IRET
      RETURN
      END
```

A call to the open-coded subroutine will now consist of a call to subroutine PUSH followed by a branch to the open-coded subroutine. Note that subroutine PUSH is not called recursively; it is simply called once each time a call to the open-coded subroutine is being made, but control is returned from PUSH as soon as the parameters and return address have been pushed down on the stack.

The main program will need to have the following initial statements:

```
      COMMON IPT, MVEC(100), NVEC(100),
    C          IRTVEC(100)
      IPT = 0
```

We may now insert statements to evaluate and print out A (2,3):

```
      CALL PUSH (2, 3, 1)
      GO TO 200
   10 WRITE (6,15) IACK
   15 FORMAT (9H A(2,3) =, I3)
      STOP
```

This assumes that the result of the recursive function will be left in IACK. Now the open-coded subroutine must be written. If the parameter M is zero, the result is $N+1$:

```
  200 IF (MVEC(IPT) .GT. 0) GO TO 211
      IACK = NVEC(IPT) + 1
      GO TO 277
```

Statement 277 will begin the return coding. Now if the parameter M is not zero, but parameter N is, the result is A ($M-1$, 1). This involves a recursive call to the open-coded subroutine. When control is returned, the value of the function as evaluated by the recursive call is the value required by the present call, and so a transfer of control to the return coding is all that is needed:

```
211 IF (NVEC(IPT) .GT. 0) GO TO 222
    CALL PUSH (MVEC(IPT)-1, 1, 2)
    GO TO 200
 20 GO TO 277
```

If neither parameter is zero, then first $A(M,N-1)$ must be evaluated. This is then used as the second parameter of another recursive call for which the first parameter is $M-1$:

```
222 CALL PUSH (MVEC(IPT), NVEC(IPT)-1, 3)
    GO TO 200
 30 CALL PUSH (MVEC(IPT)-1, IACK, 4)
    GO TO 200
 40 CONTINUE
```

Finally the coding for return from the open-coded subroutine must be written:

```
277 IRT = IRTVEC(IPT)
    IPT = IPT - 1
    GO TO (10, 20, 30, 40), IRT
    END
```

This program could be made more efficient by eliminating statements 20 and 40, and changing the computed GO TO to

```
    GO TO (10, 277, 30, 277), IRT
```

but it has been left in its present form to show the similarity between all four calls to the recursive procedure.

Queues

A queue is a list of items held in such a way that the items are retrieved in the same order as that in which they were stored. It is often known as a first-in-first-out list. In the case of a stack, items are always added and taken away from the same end, leaving the other end unchanged. With a queue, items are added at one end and removed from the other. This may be implemented in Fortran by means of a vector and two pointers, one pointer indicating the head of the queue (the next item to be removed) and the other indicating the tail (the last item which was stored). When the queue is given its first item, both pointers will refer to the beginning of the vector. As items are added and removed, the two pointers will move along the vector, the head following the tail.

At any one time the number of useful items in the queue may be small, but the vector must be long enough to accommodate all the items at one time, even though they do not need to be stored all together. This is obviously a very inefficient use of space. An alternative method would be to move the whole queue down to the beginning of the vector every time an item is removed from it, but this would be very inefficient in terms of execution time.

A better method is to use a *circular buffer*. This again consists of a vector and two pointers to the head and the tail, but the vector may be imagined as bent round until its ends meet. When the queue has travelled down to the end of the vector, it crosses the seam and re-uses the same space. Now the vector only needs to be of sufficient length to accommodate the largest size of queue which will be held at any one time.

As an example, let us consider a vector IVEC with two pointers LHD and LTL for the head and the tail respectively. The convention used here will be that when the queue is empty then the head pointer is set to zero. This will be the starting condition:

```
DIMENSION IVEC(100)
DATA LHD, LTL /2 * 0/
```

In order to add an item to the tail of the queue the following steps must be followed:

(1) Increment the tail pointer.
(2) If the tail pointer is outside the range of the vector, set it back to 1 (i.e. cross the seam).
(3) If the two pointers are now equal, the queue has overflowed, and the tail is in danger of overwriting the head.
(4) Otherwise, insert the new item at the tail of the queue.
(5) If the head pointer is zero (i.e. if this is the first item to be placed in an empty queue) set the head pointer equal to the tail pointer.

In terms of Fortran statements in the context of the initial statements given above, these steps are:

```
      LTL = LTL + 1
      IF (LTL .GT. 100) LTL = 1
      IF (LTL .NE. LHD) GO TO 10
      WRITE (6,99)
   99 FORMAT (27H ***QUEUE HAS OVERFLOWED***)
```

```
      STOP
  10 IVEC(LTL) = IVAL
     IF (LHD .EQ. 0) LHD = LTL
```

Here the value contained in IVAL is placed on the tail of the queue.

The steps needed to remove a value from the head of the queue are as follows:

(1) If the head pointer is zero, an error has occurred in attempting to remove a value from an empty queue.

(2) Take the value from the head of the queue.

(3) If the two pointers are equal (i.e. if the queue only had one value) make the queue empty by setting the head pointer to zero.

(4) Otherwise, increment the head pointer, and if it is now outside the range of the vector, set it back to 1 (i.e. cross the seam).

The Fortran statements needed to remove a value in terms of the example above are:

```
      IF (LHD .GT. 0) GO TO 20
      WRITE (6,999)
  999 FORMAT (28H ***QUEUE HAS UNDERFLOWED***)
      STOP
   20 IVAL = IVEC (LHD)
      IF (LHD .NE. LTL) GO TO 30
      LHD = 0
      GO TO 40
   30 LHD = LHD + 1
      IF (LHD .GT. 100) LHD = 1
   40 CONTINUE
```

Note that when the queue becomes empty, LTL is left with its current value. If a value is then added to the tail, the queue will contain one item again, and both LHD and LTL will be set to the incremented version of LTL.

An example of the situation in which queues are necessary is in the production of concordances, where each word in the input text produces an output line in which this word is centred in its context. When a word is read in, it must wait until sufficient of its following context has been read before it can be output. The following context may also contain words which will be output when their context is complete, and so on. The simplest way to cope with this is to use a circular buffer as a queue in which to hold the characters. If the vector is long enough, the tail of the queue can be allowed to overwrite the head continuously, as by that time the head no longer contains useful information. A head pointer is not needed in this case, and the queue never becomes empty.

Double-ended queues

A double-ended queue (or *deque*) is a queue in which items can be added or removed from either end. Its function therefore encompasses both the stack and the queue. In Fortran, a deque can be held as a vector and two pointers, just as with a queue. The methods described in the last section for adding an item to the tail and removing an item from the head may still be used here without change. Extra procedures are needed for adding a value to the head or removing a value from the tail.

In order to add a value to the head of the deque the following steps must be taken:

(1) Decrement the head pointer.

(2) If the head pointer is now negative, the deque was empty, and the value may be stored in the first place of the vector.

(3) If the head pointer is zero, set it to point to the end of the vector.

(4) If the head and tail pointers are now equal, then the deque has overflowed. Otherwise the value may be stored at the head.

The Fortran example of the last section needs the following statements to be able to do this:

```
      LHD = LHD - 1
      IF (LHD) 60, 70, 80
   60 LTL = 1
      LHD = 1
      GO TO 90
   70 LHD = 100
   80 IF (LHD .NE. LTL) GO TO 90
      WRITE (6,99)
      STOP
   90 IVEC(LHD) = IVAL
```

In order to remove a value from the tail of a deque one must follow these steps:

(1) If the head pointer is zero, then an error has occurred in attempting to remove a value from an empty deque.

(2) Take the value from the tail of the deque.

(3) If the pointers are equal, then there was only one value in the deque, and it is now empty, so set the head pointer to zero.

(4) Otherwise, decrement the tail pointer, and if necessary, cross the seam.

Again in terms of the Fortran example above, this is:

```
        IF (LHD .GT. 0) GO TO 110
        WRITE (6,999)
        STOP
  110   IVAL = IVEC(LTL)
        IF (LHD .NE. LTL) GO TO 120
        LHD = 0
        GO TO 130
  120   LTL = LTL - 1
        IF (LTL .EQ. 0) LTL = 100
  130   CONTINUE
```

Exercises

(1) In order to transform an expression from the usual form, e.g.

$$A+(B+C)*E-F$$

into the parenthesis-free reverse Polish form, e.g.

$$A\ B\ C+E*+F-$$

it is necessary to have two stacks, which we may call the output stack and the operator stack. Items are taken from the card and subjected to the following algorithm. For this purpose the end of the expression is considered one of the operators.

(*a*) Get the next item from the input.

(*b*) If the item is a variable, push it down on the output stack and return to (*a*).

(*c*) If the item is '(', push it down on the operator stack and return to (*a*).

(*d*) If the item is ')', pop the items from the operator stack and push them down on the output stack until a '(' is encountered in the stack; pop this but do not push it down on the output stack, and then return to (*a*).

(e) The item is an operator. If it has higher priority than the one on top of the operator stack, or if the operator stack is empty, push it down on the operator stack and go to (g).

(f) Pop the top of the operator stack, push the freed operator down on the output stack, and return to (e).

(g) If the top of the operator stack contains the symbol for the end of the expression, then the output stack may be written out (as a vector, and not as a stack); otherwise return to (a).

Write a program to produce the reverse Polish forms of expressions. The expressions should be punched one per card, and should use only single character variables and operators. If the expression is not permitted to contain embedded blanks, the first blank encountered can be used to indicate the end of the expression. The symbol '(' should be given higher priority than all other operators, and the end of expression should be lowest in priority.

(2) The towers of Hanoi is a famous children's game which uses three vertical rods and a number of discs. The discs all have different diameters, and have holes through the middle so that they will fit on the rods. The game starts with all the discs on one rod, and ends when they have all been transferred to another rod. Only one disc may be moved at a time, and at no time may a disc rest on one smaller than itself. Write a program to print out what moves should be made in order to transfer five discs from rod one to rod three.

This problem becomes very much simpler if one puts it into recursive form. To transfer five discs from rod one to rod three, first move four discs from rod one to rod two, then move the fifth disc from rod one to rod three, then move the four discs from rod two to rod three. To move four discs from rod one to rod two, first move three discs from rod one to rod three, then . . .

(3) A piece of text in a natural language is punched on successive cards. Write a program which will produce a word concordance of this text, i.e. for every word in the input text, a line of output will be produced with that word in the centre of it, and the maximum amount of context on either side of it. Multiple blanks occurring in the input should be reduced to one blank (e.g. at the end of each card). The context should not be limited to text which is on the same card as the word.

Use a circular buffer to queue the characters from the cards. At the beginning of the program, and when the last card has been packed into the circular buffer, half a line of blank characters should be inserted

into the buffer, as in these cases the context would otherwise be insuffi-
cient. Do not attempt to sort the concordance lines before printing them.

(4) Repeat exercise (3), but this time for data which has a sequence
number punched in the last few columns of each card. Your program
should this time print out the word in its context, and also at the end of
the line print the sequence number of the card on which the word has
been found. Note that by the time the circular buffer contains sufficient
context for one word, another card will probably have been read, and
the sequence number of the first card will be lost unless you have saved
it. In fact, a circular buffer is needed for the sequence numbers, with
pointers to the circular buffer of characters to show at what point a
particular sequence number becomes applicable.

7 List processing

Stacks and queues are useful ways of keeping certain information which ebbs and flows in an unpredictable way, yet must be kept in a fixed order. However, it is not possible to insert information into the middle of a stack or queue: items must be added and removed only at the ends. Also each stack or queue needs one or more vectors which are constant in length, even though only part of them is in use at any one time.

Situations arise which call for a more flexible method of holding information. Sometimes lists of items must be kept in linear order and yet must be capable of amendment by inserting other items into the middle of a list. Several lists may need to be stored, any one of which may be very large at one instant, and yet the total space required may always be within the capacity of the computer. The relation which exists between the data items may not be simply that of linear order, but may need to be represented by a branching tree structure. These requirements may all be provided for by means of list processing techniques.

It is not necessary to have a large corpus of specialised subroutines in order to be able to use list processing in Fortran; nor is it necessary to have some routines in Assembler language. Most list processing needs are easily supplied by writing a simple purpose-built system directly in Fortran. In fact, because of the complexity which list processing can bring, it is often preferable to write a simple system which one can easily control and understand rather than use someone else's system which has more power and sophistication than is required.

Chained lists

A chained list is most simply held in Fortran by means of two vectors, one being used for the data values and the other for pointers which chain the list together. Each element of the pointer vector contains the index of the next value in the list.

Let us consider an elementary example of this. A list of floating point values is to be kept, and values are to be inserted or removed at any point in that list. The maximum length of the list will not exceed 500 values. The two vectors needed will be set up by the statement:

```
DIMENSION LINK(500), DATUM(500)
```

The list will be held as a set of pairs of cells, one from DATUM and one from LINK. The DATUM cell will hold the value, and the LINK cell will hold the index of the next pair of cells. Such a pair of computer cells will be called a *list processing cell*. The end of the list will have a LINK cell containing zero. A short list of this type is shown in fig. 9. The list starts at position 5. The six values in the list are chained together, and consist of cells 5, 1, 3, 6, 4, and 2, i.e. the values 2.0, 5.2, 1.1, 4.8, 6.3 and 3.5 in that order. A variable must be used to keep the starting point of the list, in this case 5. The value at position 7 could be inserted between cells 3 and 6 in the list by the statements:

```
LINK(7) = LINK(3)
LINK(3) = 7
```

When a value is added to the list, a pair of cells must be allocated to hold this value and its pointer. When a value is removed from the list, the pair of cells which is freed can then be re-allocated for another purpose. Cells may be freed at any point in the vector, and not just at the ends of linear lists, as with stacks and queues. Therefore some special means must be adopted for keeping track of the cells which are free for allocation. The most effective means of doing this in Fortran is by using an available space list. This is itself a chained list, and has in it all the list processing cells which are currently free. A cell is allocated by detaching it from the available space list, and linking it into the list for which it is required. When a cell is detached from a list, it is linked into the available space list again.

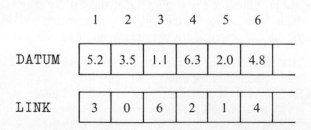

Figure 9

In the example given above the program must at the outset link all cells together into the available space list. This may be done by the statements:

```
      DO 1 I = 1, 499
    1 LINK(I) = I + 1
      LINK(500) = 0
```

Now a pointer is needed to the beginning of the available space list:

```
      LTAVSP = 1
```

Let us consider how a list can be built up by allocating cells from the available space list. The list to be built must have a pointer to the beginning of it, which will be initially zero to indicate that the list is empty:

```
      LIST = 0
```

If a floating point number contained in VAL is to be added to the beginning of the list (i.e. pushed down on the list as a stack), then the following statements are required:

```
C IF THE AV. SP. LIST IS EMPTY, GO TO
C        ERROR EXIT
       IF (LTAVSP .EQ. 0) GO TO 999
C GET A FREE CELL FROM THE AV. SP. LIST
       NEXT = LTAVSP
C MOVE ON THE AV. SP. LIST POINTER
       LTAVSP = LINK(LTAVSP)
C LINK THE FREED CELL AT THE TOP OF THE LIST
       LINK(NEXT) = LIST
       LIST = NEXT
C INSERT THE DATA VALUE
       DATUM(NEXT) = VAL
```

If the value following the beginning of the list (i.e. the second item on the list) is to be removed, the following statements will do this, and will return the cell which is freed to the available space list:

```
C IF THE LIST IS EMPTY, GO TO ERROR EXIT
       IF (LIST .EQ. 0) GO TO 999
C TAKE THE POINTER OF THE FIRST ITEM
       NEXT = LINK(LIST)
C IF THERE IS NO SECOND ITEM, GO TO
```

```
C          ERROR EXIT
      IF (NEXT .EQ. 0) GO TO 999
C BYPASS THE SECOND ITEM IN THE LIST
      LINK(LIST) = LINK(NEXT)
C RESTORE THE FREED CELL TO THE AV. SP. LIST
      LINK(NEXT) = LTAVSP
      LTAVSP = NEXT
```

In such a case as this, subroutines may be written to perform such basic tasks as taking a cell from the available space list, returning a cell which has been freed, pushing down a value on a list, etc. These will each be only a few statements in length.

In the above example it would be awkward and inefficient to add a value to the end of a list, because it would be necessary to chain down the list to find where the end is. If the task being performed requires frequent access to both ends of lists, then it is worth while keeping two pointers for every list, one of them pointing to the head and the other to the tail. This makes it much easier to perform such processes as chaining together two lists. If two lists *A* and *B* have head and tail pointers, LISTA1, LISTA2, LISTB1 and LISTB2 respectively, then the second list can be attached to the end of the first list simply by the assignments:

```
      LINK(LISTA2) = LISTB1
      LISTA2 = LISTB2
```

In the same way lists or parts of lists can be returned to the available space list without having to return them a cell at a time.

It is possible for a list processing cell to contain more than one data item if this is required. All that is needed is one or more extra vectors to hold the extra data items.

Doubly chained lists

The chained lists described in the last section can only be processed in a forward direction, i.e. one may link from a cell to its successor, but not vice versa. Sometimes this is a disadvantage. In that case, doubly chained lists may be used. This means that two vectors are used for pointers, one being for pointers to succeeding cells and the other for pointers to preceding cells. The available space list still needs to be chained only in a forward direction, as it is never necessary to access this list in a backward direction.

Let us consider an example in which the vectors are LINKF for the forward links, LINKB for the backward links, and DATUM for the data values. An example of a doubly chained list using these three vectors is shown in fig. 10. If the variable LIST1 contains a pointer to the beginning of the list, then a value contained in VAL may be pushed down at the head of the list by means of the statements:

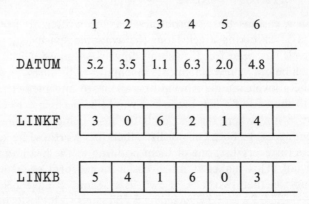

Figure 10

```
IF (LTAVSP .EQ. 0) GO TO 999
NEXT = LTAVSP
LTAVSP = LINKF(LTAVSP)
LINKF(NEXT) = LIST1
IF (LIST1 .NE. 0) LINKB(LIST1) = NEXT
LINKB(NEXT) = 0
LIST1 = NEXT
DATUM(NEXT) = VAL
```

Here, as in the last section, LTAVSP is the pointer to the available space list, and 999 is the label of an error exit. If you have difficulty in understanding what is happening in the piece of Fortran coding given here, the best plan is to take a piece of paper, a pencil and an eraser, and 'play at computers' obeying the statements one by one.

It should be apparent from the example above that processing using doubly chained lists is very similar to that using singly chained ones. The process is more complicated, however, because two pointers must be kept up to date instead of one. If the particular application does not need to chain through lists backwards, it is much safer to stay with singly chained lists.

Trees

If two vectors are used for the pointers, and if both the pointers for each cell point forwards, then each list processing cell has two successors. By this means it is possible to store data in the form of a tree which has exactly two branches at every node. If an available space list is needed, then it should again be kept in the form of a singly chained list. For an example of this aspect of list processing the reader should see the monkey-puzzle sort in chapter 8.

Sometimes the need is to be able to store data in tree form, but not a tree which has exactly two branches from every cell. If the tree has no more than two branches from any node, then two vectors of pointers may be used, but when a branch is not required, one of the pointers may be set to zero. This can be wasteful of space if the number of branches is relatively small. Another method is possible if the data vector is integer in type. In this case only one vector of pointers is required. When a branch is needed, then both the data cell and the pointer cell contain pointers. Some indication must be given that the data cell contains a pointer and not data. A convenient signal is to reverse the sign of the corresponding pointer cell. If a many-way branch is needed, then a succession of these two-way branching cells may be used.

Complications arise when deleting a tree structure, as it cannot be returned to the available space list in branched form. One solution is to strip the structure, deleting each cell separately. This is a sure method, but inefficient.

Other structures more complicated than trees may be stored using list processing techniques. Different lists may have a common branch, or sublist. A list may be circular. Such sophistications require special care when processing and deleting lists, and are best avoided if this is at all possible. If they cannot be avoided, then the system to be used must be worked out in great detail before programming begins. This is also necessary when using a ready-made list processing package.

It should be noted that more powerful means of holding data structures use successively more pointers. A stack needs one pointer, a queue two, a simply chained list n where n is the length of the list, a doubly chained list $2n$, and so on. Before a complex list processing system is used, one should be certain that there will be savings to offset the space needed for storing all the pointers.

Exercises

(1) Write a program to read in expressions in reverse Polish notation

(see exercise (1), chapter 6) and restore them to parenthesised form. The following algorithm may be used:

(*a*) Set up a simply chained list whose data items are pointers to other lists; each other list will initially consist of one item from the reverse Polish expression.

(*b*) If the list of lists has only one item on it, go to (*d*).

(*c*) Search along the list of lists until a list is found which consists of just one operator. Take the two preceding lists, surround each one with parentheses, and link them together with the operator between, making one list out of the three. Return to (*b*).

(*d*) Transfer the single list remaining to a line buffer and print it out.

(2) A large sparse array is to be held by list processing techniques. Two vectors will be used to hold pointers to the rows and to the columns. If a row or a column is entirely zero, the corresponding pointer will be zero. Otherwise the pointer will be to the start of a chained list of cells, each cell containing four items. One item is a pointer to the next cell in this row, the second is a pointer to the next cell in this column, the third contains the subscripts (the row and column) packed together, and the fourth contains a data value. Write and test subprograms to retrieve and insert values.

(3) Read in a Fortran program segment (a main program, subroutine or function) and print it out, numbering each statement. After the program segment, print each Fortran name which has been used in the segment together with a list of the numbers of all the statements in which it has been used (i.e. a cross-reference listing of all the occurrences of the names).

(4) Write a set of subroutines to handle multiprecision integers, each integer being stored as a chained list of decimal digits. Your subroutines should include those to add and print out such numbers. Multiplication is an interesting problem, and division only for the adventurous! Before writing any subroutines, consider carefully how you will hold the numbers, e.g. in what order you will store the digits, whether a doubly or singly chained list is needed, whether a separate cell for the length would be worth the extra space required, how you are going to handle negative integers. A set of functions would be more convenient to use than a set of subroutines. Why is it not possible to write functions for these purposes? Apart from the ease of printing, there is no reason why each cell should be limited to storing a decimal digit.

8 Sorting

It is only possible to touch the fringe of this enormous subject here. It may be contended that it would be better to bypass the subject entirely rather than to give such an unrepresentative survey of it. On the other hand, one commonly meets programmers who need to do some sorting and who have little knowledge of the basic algorithms available. This chapter is intended to teach such people some useful methods, and to give an indication of the situations where each method can be used.

Exchange sort

The exchange sort is the simplest method to understand, but also the least efficient in operation. It is only included here because it is the method most programmers are familiar with, and may therefore be used as a basis for comparison.

If a vector contains numbers which are to be sorted into ascending numerical order, the exchange method is to search through the whole vector for the smallest number, and then to exchange it with the number in location 1. A search is then made for the smallest number in the vector excluding location 1, and this is then exchanged with the number at location 2, and so on.

Let us suppose that a vector has been set up by the statement

```
      DIMENSION A(100)
```

and has been filled with values. In order to sort it by the exchange method the following statements are needed:

```
      DO 20 I = 1, 99
C SELECT THE FIRST ITEM AS THE POTENTIAL
C         SMALLEST
      MIN = I
C SEARCH FOR THE SMALLEST VALUE
      J = I + 1
      DO 10 K = J, 100
```

```
      IF (A(K) .LT. A(MIN)) MIN = K
   10 CONTINUE
C NOW EXCHANGE THE SMALLEST FOUND
      B = A(I)
      A(I) = A(MIN)
   20 A(MIN) = B
```

Note that in this piece of program the index of the smallest item is kept in MIN until the remainder of the vector has been scanned. Only then is an exchange performed. This method is often written in a much less efficient way. Whenever a smaller element is found, instead of its index being kept, it is then and there exchanged. This means that a large number of exchanges take place, as against only 99 exchanges in the program above.

The inefficiency of the exchange method lies in the number of comparisons which must be performed. If there are n items to be sorted, this method results in approximately $\frac{1}{2}n^2$ comparisons.

Ripple sort

This is also known as the *bubble sort*. It is quite a simple method, easily coded, and is most efficient if the data are almost in the right order at the start.

The method is to pass through the set of items repeatedly, comparing adjacent values. If two adjacent items are out of order, they are exchanged. The process stops when a pass has been made through the data with no exchanges being required.

One modification is needed to make the process more efficient. If the data are being sorted into ascending order, after one pass the largest item will be at the end of the vector, having (as it were) ridden on the crest of the wave, and having been involved in every exchange since it was first encountered. This means that the next pass through the data need not go as far as the last item. Each pass can be foreshortened by one location.

The following statements will sort the vector A used in the last section into ascending order using the ripple sort:

```
      DO 20 I = 1, 99
C SET A LIMIT ON THE PASS THROUGH THE DATA
      J = 100 - I
C SET A FLAG TO INDICATE NO EXCHANGES
```

```
C         HAVE OCCURRED
          MARK = 0
          DO 10 K = 1, J
          KP1 = K + 1
          IF (A(K) .LE. A(KP1)) GO TO 10
C EXCHANGE TWO ITEMS AND SET THE FLAG
          B = A(KP1)
          A(KP1) = A(K)
          A(K) = B
          MARK = 1
       10 CONTINUE
C TEST IF ANY EXCHANGES HAVE BEEN MADE
          IF (MARK .EQ. 0) GO TO 30
       20 CONTINUE
       30 CONTINUE
```

There are three common errors in programming the ripple sort. One is to fail to realise that the loop can be foreshortened each time. Another is to initialise the flag to zero too early in the program, so that it is not reset to zero if another pass needs to be made through the data. The other error is to forget that adjacent items may be equal, in which case no exchange must be made. Each of these errors can gravely affect the execution time of the sort. In particular, if the first error is combined with either of the other two, then infinite looping can result.

If the data to be sorted are already in order, then n items require only $n-1$ comparisons by this method. On the other hand, if the items are in exactly the reverse order, approximately $\frac{1}{2}n^2$ comparisons and exchanges will be made, which is as inefficient as the worst possible exchange method. This method is quite a satisfactory one if only a small amount of data are to be sorted, or if the data are almost in order. It has the advantage that no extra array space is needed apart from that occupied by the data. Certain refinements may be made to improve the efficiency in certain cases, e.g. sweeping alternately forwards and backwards through the data. Examples of modified ripple sorts are given in exercises (1) and (2) at the end of this chapter.

Tournament sort

The tournament sort is a method which is efficient and whose speed is completely independent of the data. Initially a hierarchy of comparisons is made, as in a tennis tournament, adjacent items being 'played' against one another, and a record kept of the winners. Adjacent winners are then played against one another, and so on until a champion is found. This situation is shown in fig. 11. The champion in the tournament is the item which should come first in the sort. This may then be printed or otherwise disposed of. In terms of the tournament analogy, it is then disqualified. Certain matches must then be replayed. These are in fact the matches in which the champion took part, one for each level of the hierarchy. At the lowest level the immediate neighbour of the champion will now win, as the champion has been disqualified. When all the replays have been performed, a new champion is found, which is the second item of the sort, and so on.

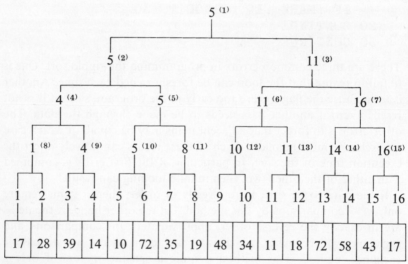

Figure 11

It will be obvious that it is most straightforward to sort items whose total number is a power of two. Several vectors of pointers are needed to keep the locations of the winners of the matches. The largest vector must be half the number of data items in length, the next a quarter, and so on. A Fortran program for this sort can be simplified if a single vector is used for all the pointers. Its length will be the number of data items minus one. In fig. 11 the numbers in parentheses indicate the indices within this vector. When two items are compared, the new index within the vector of pointers (at which a pointer to the winner must be stored) can be found by dividing either of the old indices by two. Items can be disqualified by setting them to an impossibly high value (if the sort is into ascending order). If N contains the index of a data item, or of a pointer to an item, the index of the neighbouring item or the neighbouring pointer can be placed in I by the statement:

$$I = N - 1 + 2 * MOD(N, 2)$$

If N is even, MOD(N,2) is zero, and the result is therefore N−1. On the other hand if N is odd, MOD(N,2) is one, and the result is N+1.

In order to sort n items, the initial setup will require $n-1$ comparisons, and the n replays will each require $\log_2(n-1)$ comparisons. The resulting number of comparisons is therefore $n\log_2(n-1)$. This is quite independent of the order of the input data. One disadvantage of the tournament sort is the extra space needed for the pointers. Another disadvantage may be the fact that the items are not re-arranged in store. It is a good method of sorting when the sorted information is to be directly printed or stored on a backup device. It can also be adapted to re-arrange the array in sorted order. For this purpose the first champion is exchanged with the item in the first place of the data array, and then two replays take place, one at the beginning of the array because the champion has been disqualified, and the other at the place where the champion used to be. If the length of the array is not a power of two, then the sort can be performed provided that the number of pointers is adequate for the next higher power of two, and if the non-existent items are considered to be disqualified from the start.

The tournament sort may be used as the initial stage of an external sort, as it may produce a 'string' of sorted items on a tape or disc file. The strings may then be merged together successively until finally all the items are in order on the backup store. When the tournament sort is being used for this purpose, a slight modification may be made. At the start, the array available is filled up with data items, presumably leaving some data items still to be read in. When a champion is disqualified, a new data item is read in to take its place in the array. Provided that the new item should follow the old champion in the sorted order, the new item can validly take part in the tournament, and the replay takes it into account. If the new item should go before the last champion, then a flag is set to mark this new item as 'dead', and it does not take part in the tournament. When all the items in the array are dead, the flags are unset, and a new string is begun. The result of this is that the strings on tape or disc are on average twice the length of the data array in store. However, most large modern computers have sort/merge programs provided for them which will perform such an external sort much more efficiently than a Fortran program.

Monkey-puzzle sort

This is sometimes known as the *list processing sort* or the *tree sort*. The method is to produce by list processing methods a binary-branching tree (resembling a monkey-puzzle tree) from which the items may be stripped in order. This is a very efficient sort if the items are in random order to begin with. It can be programmed in just a few lines of Fortran, but it is particularly difficult to understand. For this reason the explanation given here will first be in pictorial terms.

Let us suppose that the items to be sorted consist of the five words COD, BEE, CAT, DOG and ANT in that order, and that they are to be placed in alphabetical order. Each item will be represented by a box containing the word, to which three smaller boxes representing pointers are attached. These pointers will be called the backtrack, the left pointer and the right pointer. If any of these are left blank, this means that they contain the null pointer (zero). This collection of boxes will in fact represent one list processing cell. The items will be added to the tree one by one. When only the first item is in the tree, the situation will be as shown in fig. 12. This first entry will form the root of the tree. The tree will be shown here upside down, so that COD will always appear at the top.

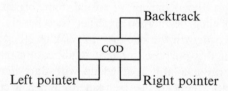

Figure 12

When the second item, BEE, is to be added to the tree, it is first compared with the item at the root. BEE precedes COD alphabetically, so the left pointer of COD will be set to point to BEE and the backtrack of BEE will point to COD. At this stage the situation is as in fig. 13. Now the third item, CAT, is added to the tree. It is first compared with the root, COD. CAT precedes COD, but COD already has a left branch, so CAT cannot be attached directly to COD. The left branch of COD is followed, and the item BEE is found. CAT is now compared with BEE; as CAT follows BEE alphabetically, the right pointer of BEE is set to point to CAT, and the backtrack of BEE is copied into the backtrack of CAT, so that they both point to COD. This situation is shown in fig. 14. In this way all five items are built into the tree, until the final situation is as shown in fig. 15.

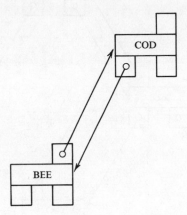

Figure 13

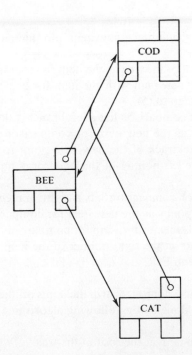

Figure 14

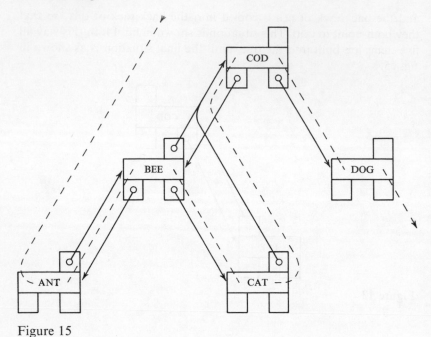

Figure 15

The algorithm for building a new item into the tree is as follows:

(1) Select the root of the tree as the item for comparison.

(2) Compare the new item with the item for comparison. If the new item should follow, go to (5).

(3) If the item for comparison has a left branch, take the item to which that branch points as the new item for comparison and go to (2).

(4) Make the backtrack of the new item point to the item for comparison, and set the left pointer of the item for comparison to point to the new item. Exit.

(5) If the item for comparison has a right branch, take the item to which that branch points as the new item for comparison and go to (2).

(6) Copy the backtrack of the item for comparison into the backtrack of the new item, and set the right pointer of the item for comparison to point to the new item. Exit.

The next thing to be done is to strip the items off the tree in the correct order. This may be done by the following algorithm:

(7) Start with the item at the root of the tree.

(8) If this item has a left branch, take the item to which that branch points and return to (8).

(9) This is the next item in order.

(10) If this item has a right branch, take the item to which that branch points and return to (8).

(11) If this item has no backtrack, exit.

(12) Take the item to which the backtrack points, and go to (9).

This algorithm may be more easily understood if it is applied to the tree in fig. 15. Numbers in parenthesis will refer to sections of the algorithm above. (7) The item COD is selected. (8) This has a left branch, so BEE is selected. (8) This has a left branch, so ANT is selected. (8) This has no left branch, so (9) ANT is the next item in order. (10) This item has no right branch, (11) but it does have a backtrack (12) which points to BEE, (9) which is the next item in order. (10) BEE has a right branch to CAT, (8) which does not have a left branch, so (9) this is the next item in order, and so on.

By following this algorithm through the tree, the items will be stripped off in the order, ANT, BEE, CAT, COD, DOG. The order in which these items are visited by the stripping-off algorithm is shown as a dotted line in fig. 15.

When programming this method, a vector is needed for the left pointers and another for the right pointers. It might appear that a third is needed for the backtracks, but this is in fact not so. No item needs both a backtrack and a right pointer at the same time. (In fig. 15 BEE has both a backtrack and a right pointer, but the backtrack is never used.) The right pointer vector can also be used to store the backtracks provided that there is some way of distinguishing between these two uses. A suitable convention which will be followed here is to store the backtrack as a negative number.

Let us now take a Fortran example. A vector A contains 100 items which must be sorted into ascending numeric order and printed out. Left pointers and right pointers will be kept in the vectors ILB and IRB respectively. No available space list is needed, as the list processing cells will be allocated in linear succession, and after the tree has been stripped all the pointers may be considered to be freed at one time. Space must be reserved for the vectors.

```
DIMENSION A(100), ILB(100), IRB(100)
```

We will now suppose that the values have been placed in A and are to be sorted. First A(1) must be placed at the root of the tree. This is done simply by making its pointers zero:

```
      ILB(1) = 0
      IRB(1) = 0
```

Now each of the other items must be placed on the tree. The labels used will be the same as the corresponding sections of the algorithms above:

```
      DO 100 I = 2, 100
      ILB(I) = 0
      IRB(I) = 0
    1 J = 1
    2 IF (A(I) .GT. A(J)) GO TO 5
    3 IF (ILB(J) .EQ. 0) GO TO 4
      J = ILB(J)
      GO TO 2
    4 IRB(I) = -J
      ILB(J) = I
      GO TO 100
    5 IF (IRB(J) .LE. 0) GO TO 6
      J = IRB(J)
      GO TO 2
    6 IRB(I) = IRB(J)
      IRB(J) = I
  100 CONTINUE
```

Now the items have all been placed on the tree. The tree must be stripped, printing the items as they are encountered in order. The most efficient way of coding this in Fortran does not allow exact correspondence with sections (7) to (12) of the algorithm above. In particular, sections (10) and (11) both correspond to the statement labelled 10 in the following program.

```
    7 J = 1
      GO TO 8
  110 J = ILB(J)
    8 IF (ILB(J) .GT. 0) GO TO 110
    9 WRITE (6,200) A(J)
  200 FORMAT (1X, F10.2)
   10 IF (IRB(J)) 12, 300, 120
  120 J = IRB(J)
      GO TO 8
   12 J = -IRB(J)
```

```
        GO TO 9
  300 CONTINUE
```

The reader is recommended to work through this program with a small amount of data, obeying the instructions in order to see how the sort takes place.

The monkey-puzzle sort needs a large amount of workspace – two cells for every item to be sorted. On the other hand it does not need to exchange the items to be sorted, and therefore it is possible to use this method to sort items of variable length such as character strings. The number of comparisons made depends on the order of the original data. If the data are already in the required order, or if it is in exactly the reverse order, then the tree will consist of only one branch, and the number of comparisons for n items will be approximately $\frac{1}{2}n^2$. If on the other hand the data are in random order, the method will approximate to a binary search with the facility of adding items to the table. The number of comparisons will be of the order of $n \log_2 n$. A further advantage of the monkey-puzzle sort is that the same data may be sorted according to several different criteria, and the results of the different sorts held at the same time in different trees.

Exercises

(1) A modified ripple sort known as a *shuttle sort* (Shaw and Trimble, 1963) works in the following way. A pass is made through the items comparing adjacent pairs. If a pair has to be exchanged, the item which was moved towards the beginning of the array is compared with the item which is now preceding it, if necessary a further exchange is made, and so on until the item has found its proper place. Only one pass need be made through the data. Write and test a subroutine to sort a vector of real numbers using this method.

(2) *Shellsort* (Boothroyd, 1963) is designed to overcome one of the shortcomings of the ripple sort, namely, that an item towards the end of the array which should be at the beginning is only moved one place towards the beginning for every pass through the data. The method is that if n items are to be sorted, then a value m is chosen which is the largest power of two less than n. A shuttle sort (see exercise (1)) is performed for each set of items which are m places apart. Then m is divided by 2, and the process repeated, until the process is done for the

last time when *m* is one. Write and test a subroutine to sort a vector of real numbers using this method.

(3) Write a subroutine to sort a vector of real numbers using a tournament sort modified so that the items are replaced in the input vector in sorted order.

(4) Use the three subroutines above to sort three sets of 1000 numbers each. The first set should consist of the numbers already in ascending order, the second set should be random, and the third set should contain the numbers in descending order. Compare the times taken for each subroutine to sort each set of data.

9 Symbol-state tables

Symbol-state tables (or *transition matrices*) use the technique of table translation described in chapter 1. The present 'state' of the program (a small positive integer) and the type of symbol encountered in the data (transformed to a small positive integer) are used to select the row and column of a table. The element of the table at this position is then used to give the new state of the program, and possibly other information also.

Symbol-state tables are particularly useful when the data must be checked for conformity to certain syntactic rules, or when the functioning of the program depends in a complex way on previous conditions. As a rule of thumb it may be taken that the kind of problem for which a symbol-state table will provide a convenient solution is one which would otherwise result in a program with a large number of IF statements. The logical complexity is taken out of the program (where it manifests itself in the numerous IF statements) and is transferred to the table. To amend the logic, the table must be changed and not the program. This means that one program can be made to apply different logical tests by reading in different tables.

Simple syntax checking

The simplest kind of symbol-state table is one whose elements contain only the next state, an error indicator, or a flag indicating that the end of a section has been reached without an error. As the states are represented by small positive integers, the error indicators may be negative integers, and the end-of-section marker may be zero.

An actual problem which was solved using this technique was to count the number of different clause types in some coded natural language material. The text had been coded to show grammatical categories, and the focus of interest was on the indirect object (IO), the subject (S) and the verb (V) in different clause types. A count was required of the clauses which fitted the eight patterns:

$$(1) \qquad \text{IO} \quad \text{S} \qquad \text{V}$$

(2)		S	IO	V
(3)		S	V	IO
(4)	IO	V	S	
(5)		V	IO	S
(6)		V	S	IO
(7)	IO	V		
(8)		V	IO	

Other elements of the clause were to be ignored for the purposes of this analysis. A diagnostic message was to be produced for clauses which did not match any of these eight types.

The proposed solution was to use the symbol-state table shown in fig. 16. The cells shown blank were in fact filled with negative numbers as error indicators. At the start of each clause the state was set to 9. A subroutine was called to find the type of the next item in the clause. If this was one of the required items, then a new state was taken from the table. When the end of the clause was reached, then if the result lay between 1 and 8, this gave the type of the clause which had just been checked. If at any time a negative number was selected from the table, or if at the end of a clause the state was greater than 8, a diagnostic message was printed.

In terms of the Fortran program, a DIMENSION statement is needed for the table, and for the counts of clause types:

```
DIMENSION ITAB(3,16), KOUNT(8)
```

The table must be filled with the values shown in fig. 16, and the counts set to zero. Now the state must be initialised before beginning to check a clause:

```
1 ISTAT = 9
```

Let us suppose that a subroutine is available which determines the type of the next item in the clause, and which sets its argument to -1 at the end of a clause, -2 at the end of the data, 1, 2 or 3 for a subject, verb or indirect object respectively, and zero otherwise.

```
2 CALL NEXT(ITP)
  IF (ITP) 10, 2, 3
```

Now the new state must be read from the table:

```
3 ISTAT = ITAB(ITP, ISTAT)
  IF (ISTAT .GT. 0) GO TO 2
```

If the control passes this point, then a diagnostic must be written out.

	S	V	IO
	1	2	3
1			
2			
3			
4			
5			
6			
7	4		
8	5		
9	10	15	13
10		11	12
11			3
12		2	
13	14	7	
14		1	
15	16		8
16			6

Figure 16

At statement 10 a test must be made to distinguish between the end of the clause (in which case ITP is −1) and the end of the data (when ITP is −2). If it is the end of a clause, then a further test must be made to see that ISTAT is no more than 8. If it is not, then KOUNT(ISTAT) may be incremented by one. If the end of the data has been encountered, then the values in the KOUNT vector must be written out.

Action calls

In many cases it is not sufficient for the table to contain new states or error codes. Often the table must also contain information concerning the action to be performed by the program when a particular stage has been reached. These pieces of information are termed *action calls*. As action calls may be needed at a place in the table which also contains a new state, the two are packed together into the one integer cell.

In chapter 5 the problem was mentioned of identifying keywords one of which is wholly contained within another, e.g. END which is contained within ENDFILE. For the sake of brevity, let us take a shorter example. Suppose that a string of characters is being scanned for occurrences of the three strings AN, AND and AT. The table in fig. 17 may be used for this, together with a subroutine which delivers the types of characters, the numerical values of the types corresponding to the columns of fig. 17. For each element of the table, the units digit is the next state, and the tens digit (if any) is an action call.

	A	D	N	T	Other
	1	2	3	4	5
1	2	0	0	0	0
2	0	0	13	30	0
3	0	20	0	0	0

Figure 17

Let us suppose that the table in fig. 17 is contained in an array defined as:

```
DIMENSION ITAB(5, 3)
```

Before a scan is performed from a particular point in the character string, a marker is set to zero to indicate that as yet none of the strings have been found. Also the initial state is set to one:

```
ISTR = 0
ISTAT = 1
```

Now a subroutine is called to deliver the type of the next character, which is then used in accessing the table:

```
1 CALL NEXT(ITP)
  ISTAT = ITAB(ITP, ISTAT)
C SEPARATE ACTION DIGIT FROM STATE DIGIT
  IACT = ISTAT/10
  ISTAT = ISTAT - 10*IACT
C IF A STRING HAS BEEN FOUND KEEP
C      ACCOUNT OF IT
  IF (IACT .GT. 0) ISTR = IACT
C TEST FOR EXIT FROM SEARCH
  IF (ISTAT .GT. 0) GO TO 1
```

When control passes from this coding, ISTR will contain 1, 2 or 3 to indicate whether AN, AND or AT was the longest string found at this point in the character string, or else it will contain zero if none of these has been identified.

In chapter 2 the problem of reading a free-format floating point number was mentioned. The syntax to be checked is quite extensive. The number may be preceded by not more than one sign. There may be no digits before the decimal point, or no digits after, but there should not be a decimal point without digits either before or after. There may or may not be an exponent. If there is, then there may be a sign following the 'E', and there must be at least one decimal digit. The table in fig. 18 is designed to drive a subroutine which will deliver the next free-format floating point number from an input stream. The number will be delimited by either a space or the end of the record. In fig. 18 the character strings to the left of the table indicate what items have been found when the table is at the state corresponding to that row. BOR is used to indicate the beginning of the record, EOR for the end of record, s for a sign, and d for a decimal digit. The action digits are multiplied by 100 when they are packed into the cells of the table. When an action call is found, a computed GO TO may be performed based on it. The action calls in this example correspond to the following processes which the Fortran program must perform:

		Digit	+	–	.	E	Blank	EOR
		1	2	3	4	5	6	7
BOR Blank	1	303	2	202	4	709	1	101
s	2	303	709	709	4	709	709	709
d	3	303	709	709	5	709	0	100
. s.	4	405	709	709	709	709	709	709
d. d.d .d	5	405	709	709	709	6	0	100
E	6	608	7	507	709	709	709	709
Es	7	608	709	709	709	709	709	709
Ed Esd	8	608	709	709	709	709	0	100
Error	9	9	9	9	9	9	0	100

Figure 18

(1) Read a new record and start at the beginning of it.

(2) Set a flag to indicate that the number is negative.

(3) Accumulate the present digit into the integral part of the number.

(4) Accumulate the present digit into the fractional part of the number, and increment a count of the number of fractional digits.

(5) Set a flag to indicate that the exponent is negative.

(6) Accumulate the present digit into the exponent.

(7) Print out an error message, and re-enter the table without moving on to the next character. (This is necessary so that when the end of record has been reached and an error found, a new record can be read in after the error has been handled.) Set the present number to 0.0.

If it is desired, action number 7 can be split up into several different actions to distinguish between different types of errors, and to print out different diagnostic messages. The table is so designed that when an error has been encountered, the rest of that number is automatically skipped, so that the number which follows can be read correctly.

Subroutine calls

If a certain sub-structure needs to be checked at more than one point in the structure of the data, then the symbol-state table may be written more compactly by using a 'subroutine'. A certain section of the table is 'called' from another part, the return state being stored. When the 'subroutine' has finished checking the sub-structure, a zero state may be used to indicate a return. Then the return state is restored, and normal table access continues.

Let us consider a hypothetical example. Words in a certain language have been punched on cards and must be proofread. The language has a very simple word structure. A word may be one or two syllables, but not more. Each syllable contains one and only one vowel ('A', 'E', 'I', 'O' or 'U'), which must be preceded by a plosive ('P', 'T' or 'K'), or by a semivowel ('Y' or 'W'), or by a plosive followed by a semivowel. The vowel of the syllable may or may not be followed by a liquid ('R' or 'L'). A table which will check the words is shown in fig. 19. The cells left blank will contain error flags. Notice that the tests for each syllable need to be applied twice over, once for the first syllable of the word, and again if there is a second syllable. For structures which are hierarchical this can cause massive reduplication of parts of the table.

A simplification is to turn the tests for a single syllable into a table subroutine, as in fig. 20, in which rows 4 to 7 are the subroutine. The hundreds digit is used here to indicate a subroutine call, when the units digit indicates the return state which must be stored. Notice that if a plosive is found in state 1, then the next state will be 4 (to test for a semi-vowel or a vowel), and the return state of 2 will be stored. However, if a semivowel is found in state 1, the subroutine can be entered at state 5. Unlike Fortran subroutines, it is possible to jump into them at any point. When a subroutine is 'called', the next symbol is taken from the input stream, just as with any normal transition from one state to another. When control is returned from a subroutine, however, the next symbol is not taken. If, for instance, a blank is encountered in state 6 when the return address is 2, then the return address is used as the new state, and the same character (the blank) is used together with state 2 to access the table. This is done because the last character checked by any table subroutine is a character not belonging to the sub-structure, and which must therefore be checked outside of the subroutine.

	P T K	Y W	A E I O U	R L	Blank	Other
	1	2	3	4	5	6
1	2	3			1	
2		3	4			
3			4			
4	6	7		5	1	
5	6	7			1	
6		7	8			
7			8			
8				9	1	
9					1	

Figure 19

	P T K	Y W	A E I O U	R L	Blank	Other
	1	2	3	4	5	6
1	402	502			1	
2	403	503			1	
3					1	
4		5	6			
5			6			
6	0	0	0	7	0	0
7	0	0	0	0	0	0

Figure 20

If action calls are used together with subroutine calls, then when the return state or new state is included, three numbers must be packed into each cell of the table, and unpacked when the table is accessed. Table subroutines may call other table subroutines, but in this case a stack is needed to hold the return states. With the addition of a stack, a table subroutine may call itself recursively. This is a very useful feature when checking structures which are themselves recursive, e.g. expressions. Further details are given in Day (1970*b*).

Building tables automatically

The main disadvantages of symbol-state tables are that the tables are tedious to construct, that large tables are needed for most practical purposes, and that most of the elements of the tables are simply error flags, and therefore the space is largely wasted.

These disadvantages can be overcome to some extent by storing the table as a virtual array, i.e. not storing the error flags, and storing all other values in a hash table as described in chapter 4, and furthermore by constructing the table automatically. If the table is a virtual array, its size may be considered as indefinitely large. If the table is designed for pattern matching of strings of characters, then the number of columns may be the number of characters available on that machine, or even the number 513 if the method of hashing characters mentioned in chapter 5 is being used. There is no penalty for using such a large number of columns, as the number of non-error cells will remain unchanged, and it is only these which are stored. When the subscripts are packed into a cell the column index should be in the low order position, so that the row index may be indefinitely large.

The method of inserting a character string into such a table is as follows. A record is kept of the next row of the symbol-state table which is completely free. The character string is matched against the table, beginning with row 1. As soon as the match fails, i.e. as soon as part of the string is reached which is not yet in the table, then a pointer is added from the present location to the next free row, and the free row count is increased. When the end of the string is reached, an action call can be added to the current cell of the table.

Exercises

(1) Write a program to check the syntax of an assembly language program. The assembly language statements are punched one per card, and consist of a label, an operation code, operands and comments. The delimiter between each of these fields is one or more spaces. The label and comments are optional. A label is simply a name, which is from one to eight alphabetic or numeric characters of which the first must be alphabetic. The operation codes ST, S and L each have as operands a register designation, a comma and a name. A register designation is an R followed by one or two decimal digits. The operation codes LR and SR take as operands two register designations separated by a comma. (Hint: the columns of your table should include those for L, R, S and T, and one for all other alphabetic characters.)

(2) Write a program to read and check a Fortran assignment statement.

(Make as many restrictions on the assignment statement as you find necessary.)

(3) Write a program to tidy up a Fortran program by replacing the labels by others which are in ascending numerical order within each program segment (i.e. within the main program, each subroutine and each function). It will be necessary to store the statements of the program segment. To save space you may ignore the trailing blanks of each statement. As you read in the statements, build up a table of the old labels with the new equivalent of each one. Then produce the modified segment a statement at a time. Besides changing the label at the start of each statement, remember that references to labels must also be changed. These can occur in a GO TO (simple, assigned or computed), a DO, an ASSIGN, an arithmetic IF, a READ or a WRITE statement. Also all of these statements apart from the DO may occur as the trailer of a logical IF. Use a symbol-state table to check for these statements. The table may also be used to record the first position of a label to be changed as it checks the syntax. Hold the statement as a chained list in order to modify the labels. (This is a very difficult problem, but uses most of the techniques mentioned in this book.)

Bibliography

Barron, D. W. (1968) *Recursive Techniques in Programming* (London).

Boothroyd, J. (1963) Shellsort. *Communications of the ACM*, **6**, 445.

Day, A. C. (1970*a*) Full table quadratic searching for scatter storage. *Communications of the ACM*, **13**, 481–2.

Day, A. C. (1970*b*) The use of symbol-state tables. *The Computer Journal*, **13**, 332–9.

Day, A. C. (1971) Fortran as a language for linguists. In *The Computer in Literary and Linguistic Research* (Cambridge) pp. 245–57.

Foster, J. M. (1967) *List Processing* (London).

Gries, D. (1971) *Compiler Construction for Digital Computers* (New York) pp. 216–24.

Haddon, E. W. and Proll, L. G. (1971) An Algol line-syntax checker. *The Computer Journal*, **14**, 128–32.

Knuth, D. E. (1968) *The Art of Computer Programming*, vol. 1 *Fundamental Algorithms* (Reading, Mass.).

Maurer, W. D. (1968) An improved hash code for scatter storage. *Communications of the ACM*, **11**, 35–8.

Moon, B. A. M. (1971) List-processing in plain Fortran. *The Australian Computer Journal*, **3**, 117ff.

Morris, J. (1969) Programming recursive functions in Fortran. *Software Age*, January, 38–42.

Morris, R. (1968) Scatter Storage Techniques. *Communications of the ACM*, **11**, 38–44.

Radke, C. E. (1970) The use of quadratic residue research. *Communications of the ACM*, **13**, 103–5.

Shaw, C. J. and Trimble, T. N. (1963) Shuttle sort. *Communications of the ACM*, **6**, 312.

Shell, D. A. (1959) A high-speed sorting procedure. *Communications of the ACM*, **2**, 30–2.

Index

A format 10
Ackerman's function 55
Action calls (for symbol-state tables) 86
Automatic table building 91
Available space list 65
Axes (for a graph) 23, 25
Bar charts 21
Basic techniques 1
Binary search 35, 43
Bit manipulation 4, 5
Bubble sort 72
Buffers 6
Chained lists 64
Character manipulation 9, 14, 43
Character to floating point conversion 18, 87
Character to integer conversion 14
Clause types 83
Collating sequence 44
Collisions (in a hash table) 38
Comparing characters 10
Conversion:
    characters to floating point numbers 18
    characters to integers 14
    integers to characters 15
DATA statement viii, 10
Density plots 30
Deques (double-ended queues) 60
DO-loops 2, 4, 5
Double-ended queues 60
Doubly chained lists 67

Exchange sort 71
Execution-time formats 17
External sort 75
Factorial 53
First-in-first-out list 57
Flags 1
Floating point numbers from characters 18, 87
Formats, execution-time 17
Graph plotting 20
Grid (for a graph) 25, 26, 33
Hash table 37, 40, 48
Hashing 37, 40, 43
Histograms 21, 36
Identifying characters 43
Identifying keywords 45
Identifying words 47
Integer to character conversion 15
Integers from characters 14
Keywords 45, 86
Last-in-first-out list 51
Line plots 27
Linear search 11, 14, 37, 40, 43, 45, 48
Lineprinters 20
Linked lists (chained lists) 64
List processing 64
List processing cells 65
List processing sort 76
MOD function 2, 43
Monkey-puzzle sort 76
Non-linear search 40
Numbers and characters 14

Open-coded subroutines 7
Packing numbers 3, 14
Point plots 24
Pointers 51
Pushdown stores 51
Queues 57
  double ended 60
Recursion 52, 91
Ripple sort 72
Scales (for a graph) 23, 25, 33
Scaling graphs 20, 24, 27, 30, 31
Searching (a table) 11, 35, 43
Shellsort 81
Shuttle sort 81
Sort/merge 75
Sorting 71
Sparse arrays 12, 37

Stacks 51
Subroutine calls (in symbol-state
  tables) 89
Subroutines, open-coded 8
Switches 1
Symbol-state tables 83
Syntax checking 83
Table lookup 35
Table translation 5, 14
Tournament sort 73
Transition matrices 83
Tree sort 76
Trees 69
Unpacking numbers 4, 15
Variable formats 17
Virtual arrays 92
Words 47